CW00522133

Imke Spilker

Translation by Kristina McCormack

EMPOWERED HORSES

Learning *Their* Way through Independence, Self-Confidence, and Creative Play

J.A. Allen • London

First published in 2009 by
J.A. Allen
45–47 Clerkenwell Green
London EC1R 0HT

J.A. Allen is an imprint of Robert Hale Ltd

www.halebooks.com

ISBN: 978-0-85131-968-1

Originally published in the German language as *Selbstbewusste Pferde* by
Animal Learn Verlag, Am Ange 36, 83233, Bernau, Germany, 2006.

Disclaimer of Liability
The author and publisher shall have neither liability nor responsibility to any person or entity with respect to any loss or damage caused or alleged to be caused directly or indirectly by the information contained in this book. While the book is as accurate as the authors can make it, there may be errors, omissions, and inaccuracies.

A catalogue record for this book is available from the British Library.

Photo credits: K. Baumbusch (59); H.-P.Gerstner (4); E. Moll (2); S. Bachmann (1); J. Pfeifer (1). All other photos: Atelier Gegenlicht (Backlight Studio), Bernd Illig, Laer

Book design by Erika Gavin
Cover design by Heather Mansfield

Printed in China

Contents

Prelude—In the Pasture

It all began when I asked myself what it might be like to be a horse—my horse. What would I think about people, about their desires, their actions? What would I think, were I my horse, about me, the one who demands to ride? Nothing flattering—or so it seemed to me.

I put the saddle down on the grass and sat next to it, feeling uncertain about what to do next. The horses looked at me out of the corners of their eyes and continued plucking at their blades of grass.

What gives you the right to do what you always do—punish what you call disobedient, try to control them, lay claim to their body? What are you doing here? Why do you do that? I began to feel unwell. I had no answers. I was tired. As I turned to go, I heard someone coming behind me. My horse was trotting along, following me.

"It's okay buddy. You're a good boy. It's just that I don't want to do this anymore. I wanted us to be friends, but somehow I've messed it up." I cleaned out my pockets and fed him whatever treats I had. As I started to leave, my horse blocked my way with his large body. "That's all for now. I don't have anything else for you." Absentmindedly, I went to make my way around him.

"Halt!"

"That's what comes of this," I thought to myself. "Now I'm hearing voices." It was late, the saddle slipped off my hip and I shifted it back into place and made an effort to banish my gloomy thoughts. I wanted to go home, but my horse stopped me in my tracks.

"Stay here, please!" Confused, I remained standing where I was. My horse had nearly pushed me over. What the...?

"Listen to me. You cannot simply walk away from this."

How different he suddenly seemed—strong, full of life, commanding respect. I swallowed, and finally stammered, "But what do you want from me? What can I possibly do?"

And that is how this book came to be.

"I will put my all into this, and give my best, so that these horses, with their friendly nature, will judge me kindly, and so that harmony reigns, carried by the total unity of two living beings."

~Nuno Oliveira

About This Book

We human beings have become accustomed to seeing animals as mute, inferior creatures, and though we may think of them and speak of them, we do not speak *with* them. But that is precisely what we will be doing here: we will talk with the horses.

"Communicating with Horses" is the name of a project begun a number of years ago on my initiative to foster understanding between people and horses (www.kommunikativepferde.de). The horses there and in this book are active equal partners, and they seek contact and understanding with human beings. They are free to express their feelings without restriction, and they can choose what they want to do. A person can talk with these horses...and can learn from them.

I have not used a rigid "how-to" manual format in this book. Rather, I have let myself be inspired by various sources. What lies before you—in seemingly good order—evolved from a time of confusing impressions, explosive experiences, and stimulating discussions, all of which I have woven into a new pattern in the text. The individual chapters follow one another in the same order that a person first creates a relationship with a horse from which a working partnership can then evolve. At the same time, each individual interaction between man and horse begins like this and carries all the same individual elements within it.

The path to the world of horses begins in our thoughts. And this book is intended as a kind of "play" of thoughts that makes it possible to enter that other world. However, no book can replace direct experience.

Where your own personal communication with a horse is concerned, there can be only two experts. One is reading this book just now. The other will know that you have read it!

"It can be ascertained that Man is the noblest of all creatures by the fact that no other creature has yet contradicted him."
~Georg Christoph Lichtenberg, 1772

"The senses are a bridge from the tangible to the intangible. Seeing plants and animals is to feel their mystery. Hearing the thunder is to feel its mystery. Understanding the language of forms is to be nearer to its mystery, Life itself."

~August Macke

When you begin to see through the eyes of horses you will enter another world. In this world, laws more ancient than ours are in effect. Existence is clear and uncomplicated. Every step into this world lets us sense more deeply, breathe more freely. A quiet rhythm encompasses this life.

INTRODUCTION: A Journey of Thoughts

A Path of Friendship

Certainly you have had the feeling, at least once in your life, of being in complete harmony—with the natural world around you, with a partner, with yourself. These are fortunate moments, ones when you feel confident, strong, and connected to everything. With no particular personal triumph involved, these are high points of life.

What lies before you in this book is an inner "path" into the world of horses. I will ask you to open yourself and do what I would ask you to do if you were standing beside me and were coming to these horses as my guest. Leave all your expectations behind. Go to the horses free. What is written in this book is maybe not something you would always want to read—perhaps it is not even what I would have most wanted to write.

Learn how to come into harmony with the horses' world—step-by-step. When you become open to their totally different viewpoint, you give their world a new reality: everything becomes more spacious, more open, more free. A relationship with horses in freedom entails discovering a piece of your own freedom too. Your thoughts will head in a new direction. You will orient yourself anew.

In Alien Hands

If we human beings want to live in harmony with horses today, it is important to give them as much freedom as possible. The relationship between humans and animals is no longer natural and in balance. Our species has become overly powerful and dominates all other life. Our relationship to nature has shifted and is out of balance: many people behave as though animals were put on the earth solely for their amusement and use.

Horses are defenseless against the relentless encroachment of human beings. To give them a sense of well being in our company, it is important to structure the relationship so they horses do not feel oppressed by our might, but rather, feel empowered by our presence. In our time, the challenge is no longer whether we will be able to dominate all other species, but instead whether we, long the victor, can find a way to exercise self-restraint toward those we have defeated. A connection with mankind could offer the horses of today the opportunity to develop themselves, to be completely themselves, to win back a bit of their lost freedom. As an alternative to losing more and more from their contact with us, horses could gain some space in which to preserve their independence even though they must live in a human world.

To the horse, a human he has come to know in an agreeable manner is an interesting, friendly, but strange creature. A horse is a horse and wants to live with other horses. He does not find he has much in common with us.

Silent Understanding

Befriended horses love to be near one another. They frequently graze side by side or doze together in harmony, one horse's head on the other's withers. They will stand close together for hours—the tail of one serving as fly protection for the other. They generously engage in mutual grooming, each nuzzling the other, or scratching him with his teeth, precisely the way he wants to be nuzzled or scratched. Horses who like one another live in harmonious unity. They adapt to one another, calm and encourage each other.

Generally horses look for such peaceful harmony only amongst themselves. Sometimes they will include a person who has lived among them for a long time. Yet, every one of us can communicate with a horse in this manner, because this kind of understanding can be learned. Adapt yourself to the silent language of horses, be fully present in the moment, mind the rhythm, become aware of the greater unity, the bond between you—and an intuitive understanding will come to be.

Horses are interwoven in the fabric of relationships on many levels and are constantly engaged in balancing these and creating harmonious equilibrium within the herd, with their natural surroundings, and even in the human sphere of influence. Let us observe such an instance.

The horse does not need us. Unlike a dog that follows people to be close to them, a horse does not compete for our love. He finds the sort of protection and companionship he needs among his own kind. His affection does not come easily and it cannot be bought. Those who seek friendship with a horse must wait until he invites them. The horse's friendship toward a guest is a gift.

A First Encounter

Look at these horses to see how they conduct themselves when first meeting in their pasture.

One wet autumn day a new member has joined the herd. He is the small grey stallion, the one still wearing a halter. The horses put their heads together, sniff each other thoroughly, and squealing once during the process in the accepted equine fashion. The newcomer—an Icelandic—has identified the leader of the herd, and "makes himself big," which does not overly impress the stronger Haflinger. The two horses play hard—they romp and pinch each other and look quite pleased doing it. In this way they get to know and check out each other's abilities. Their mock fighting is a kind of game of "mirrors"—the movement of one being reflected by the movement of the other, and this creates closeness between them and makes them friends. After a time, they adapt more and more, and in the end, an understanding prevails, visible even from a distance and in movement. "Why fight? There is plenty of space and food for everyone."

Meeting freely like this in a field, horses test each other through play. "Who are you?" "How leader-like, how patient, how clever are you?" There are three stallions in this group, but the encounter is free of aggression or competitive fighting. The primary interest of these horses is not apparently herd hierarchy. After a while, the Haflinger lets the smaller and younger newcomer assume the lead; he has satisfied himself as to the other's qualities. The changeover was not at all obvious, and by the way, would have been barely noticed by an observer. The central point of the horses' activity is not who is leader of the moment but whether harmony among them is achieved. The photos let you follow the process. First the two horses face off and alternately incite one another. Back and forth it goes like a ball game—rhythm, pace, and technique—all are varied frequently.

Then the horses begin to move together and play shoulder to shoulder until, finally, they trot away together, perfectly in synch like two longtime pasture pals.

Here we stand, clueless. Each of us is looking in a different direction. What can I do to come to an understanding with my horse? How do I bridge the distance between man and horse that makes our being together so difficult? Is a friendship like the one that exists between horses even possible? Are not man and horse too different and their respective interests too one-sided?

Emotional Experts

To see the world through another's eyes, to experience it as he does, is often difficult for us even when we love another person and very much want to do it.

Horses do this more easily. They sense the disposition of the other, and effortlessly "read" his physical expression, even from a distance. Horses feel when they see. They pay less attention to individual details like the face or voice, and take in the energy radiating from the whole being. A horse has only his body and movement with which to live out his tensions, his emotions. Even when he whinnies loudly because he feels alone, his whole body is involved in making the sound.

Sensing the feelings of another, going within oneself, and participating or engaging with others—these modalities have become highly specialized methods of perception among horses, such as can be found only in exceptionally gifted people in our culture. Horses know the state of their rider—often far better than the rider himself. Their empathetic perception encompasses human beings because horses share a common language with us, a language that in the beginning was also our only one, wordless, universal, written in our "gut"—the language of the body.

Nevertheless, the encounter between human and horse is more difficult than between one horse and another. Since I, the human being, unilaterally arranged the fact that we are together, I am responsible for how things go. So, let us, in our thoughts, open ourselves to how this situation appears to a horse. A true understanding of the other, be he person or animal, is only possible if I make the effort to see things from his point of view. How is my horse feeling?

How does he behave with other horses? What can I do so that he feels similarly comfortable in my presence?

Horseplay

Interestingly, there is no concept in our language for the kind of overriding agreement or harmonious unity that occurs in certain situations: within an intimate, trusting group it sometimes happens that all members participate as equals and both lead and follow. A unique dynamic can occur at play, while singing or dancing—one that knows neither follower nor leader—because what happens between the individual participants becomes a greater "whole." Togetherness teaches a kind of rhythm of feeling that all participants experience. The power of interaction and the collective act define what occurs, though our language lacks the words to describe this.

Observe the interactive rhythm of the two horses in the photos on pages 8 and 9. When the young stallions first meet, it is the bay who initiates contact. A heated squabble ensues, conducted according to the principle "as you do to me, I'll do to you." Then the grey is inspired to cool off in the pond after all the "horsing around." His bay opponent finds this idea pretty cool and also goes into the water. Again, the two of them adapt their actions to one another. Back on land, they both have a wallow in the very same spot, which is not likely the most comfortable place because of the branch lying there. The bay has once again started things and his friend follows suit. The final dust bath is like a mirror image.

Horseplay

Two young stallions enjoying themselves: First they greet each other. Then they alternate activities. They play: wrestling and fighting games, always in a circle. Not only the play, but also subsequent behavior shows an overriding understanding between them. Whether pawing, bathing, wallowing—they both initiate actions and inspire the other. Their interaction is defined by mutuality, but at the same time allows for individual needs and ideas.

Horses like harmony. They have a preference for social behaviors that arise from precise mutual attunement. Each horse takes up the stimulating suggestions of the other, performs the friend's actions himself, and as a result, a physical connection comes to be, an image of oneness. Horses have a pronounced sense of harmoniously synchronized movement sequences. They act in unison, groom one another, motivate each other and run in rhythm—this is the principle of the herd.

A moment ago he was still playing. Now I am offering him my companionship. I am trying to establish a connection, to come close to him—equal to equal. This way we can start a conversation, take up contact with one another. "Let's do something together."

Ready for Conversation

"Hey, you!"

I want to reduce the distance between us, but it would be disrespectful to push my way into the horse's personal space and touch him, without first asking permission. Think of the same situation in human terms: if I want to convince a person I don't know about my finer qualities and meet him in a spirit of friendship, I'll wait for his invitation, or offer one myself. People that do not abide by this rule of politeness can seem aggressive, even when they don't intend to be. So, when we respect a horse's personal space we convey the message, "I come as a friend."

Nurturing the relationship according to the horse's rules and in the horse's rhythm, I try, despite all our differences, to show my affection, to offer myself to the horse as a friend, as a companion.

Are these two horses racing, or running together? "A horse race" has become almost synonymous with intense competition, from a human perspective. Here, though, the grey is easily the superior "competitor" in that he far surpasses the little bay in strength and speed. But, he lets the bay run on the shorter inside track, while he himself takes the outside so that his friend can easily keep pace with him.

Horses in Resonance

Two horses are running. Is it a race, head to head? The bay gelding in the lead is weaker, smaller, lower in the herd hierarchy, and actually slower, but are these distinctions really important here? Whether one horse is higher or lower, up or down—the two horses are moving totally in unison. Their gallop strides flow smoothly, they are running in harmony, synchronized. Their shared rhythm carries and strengthens both of them, making their running light and effortless. You may know the effect from the field of acoustics—it's the law of resonance. When a note sounds in a room and causes one of the strings of a piano to vibrate, a sound will suddenly emanate from the piano. Movement, too, creates resonance.

What looks to a casual observer like a race between competing animals is in reality a unified form, a distinct entity, a unique whole. Horses very much like to run in this way. They have a very strongly defined sense of harmonious movement sequences—whether trotting at the front of a carriage, or in play as shown here—they go along with one another, become one in movement. They create a kind of symphony of movement.

Have you ever observed the flight of wild geese? Each bird flies in such a way that he "melts" with all the others into a defined shape. That way, the flap of each individual bird's wings strengthens the combined energy of the whole flock. Overriding unity like this makes the work of flying easier. It conserves the energy reserves. Not only do individual geese give each other strength as they fly in formation, they also draw some energy from the space surrounding them. The harmony of the group provides added power for the long flight. Their identical, attuned movement works like an invisible net, its threads made of energy that connects one bird to the other and creates a greater whole—thus providing added benefits to all.

Synergy

Movement in unity, on one wavelength: this is how many types of animals cover great distances and achieve the extraordinary. They melt into an entirety that is more powerful than they are individually.

We humans, too, know of such unifying experiences—the sports team that all of a sudden plays fantastically well, as though taken over by a special spirit. One current flows through all the players—everything happens as if on its own, all sense the same rhythm, and they achieve the unimaginable. In sports, they say the team is on a streak, or a winning run. Or, there is the heightened state of being in love: two people come together in overriding unity and feel as though they have been given wings—connected, yet free; individuals, yet together as one, carried by an all-encompassing melody. These are moments of joy that one never forgets.

"One cannot see the light. It is what makes us see."
~Henry Corbin

The harmonious interplay of free beings allows something new to come into existence. There is an increase of energy that everyone can suddenly feel. That alone is an exciting process. But when, in addition, the participants are as different from one another as a person and a horse—well, on the following pages you will discover what happens!

It would be best if you read the next section of the book outdoors—perhaps in the pasture. Take the book with you for a quiet walk on a sunny day. Sit in the grass near some horses, and observe them.

The kind of togetherness that leads to feelings of resonance can also exist between a horse and a human being, even over a fence. The overriding unity encompassing these two is visible in their synchronized leaps. Such an encounter has a magic all its own. Their common activity connects these two beings who come from totally different ways of life. Their joy in one another determines what happens, creates the form, and allows spontaneous harmony to arise.

Horse Imaginings

Here is an Icelandic horse in his meadow. It is autumn, and he was able to spend the whole summer like this, under the open sky, in large pastures, with the company of the herd. Many horses would be thankful to be able to enjoy even a few hours a day of such joyful freedom. Simply to be outdoors is a privilege for the horse of today.

This young stallion lives with his friends in nearly natural surroundings. It is a lovely, carefree existence. But, he must also live in the human world, which greatly circumscribes his freedom. People fence him in, burn their mark on him, and control the course of his life. It is not up to him what food he eats, which path he takes, who his companions are, which mares he wins, or even whether he will produce offspring. Self-determination has been taken from him, his future lies in the hands of strangers, and he cannot influence it. We human beings run his life.

From our point of view this is necessary—but what about from the horse's point of view? What does such an animal, whose forebears roamed the endless steppes for millions of years, feel about this? Where does his spirit dwell? There he stands at the fence...

There is an entryway. Once you go through it, you will never again be able to distance yourself from the concerns of horses. You will no longer be deaf to their language. You will no longer be unreceptive to their feelings. It is up to you to take this step. We invite you into the world of horses. Come with us now to the other side...

And Allah took a handful of the south wind,

breathed into it and created the horse

"You I have created without compare.

All the treasures of the world lie between

your eyes.

Virtue is braided into the hair of your forelock...

I have given you the power to fly

without wings and triumph without Sword..."

~Ancient Bedouin legend

There you are! Welcome! I am Reno of Stonebrook, leader of the communicative horses here, and I am pleased to see you. It is not my nature to say much. I would rather leave that to her—the author! But, as the mentor and spiritual head of this project, I will be glancing your way occasionally in the course of the book. Look at us, pay more attention to the pictures than to words, and trust your feelings.

The World of Horses

In the Beginning...

One does not have to go far to meet horses. During a walk in the country we can see them grazing peacefully on the other side of a fence. We stay with them for a while and stroll on. Or, we yield to a group of riders coming toward us. They sit on the sweating bodies of these animals. There is laughter and a restless tossing of horses' heads. Horses and people. Even in our car-crowded cities, we do not have to go far to find horses. They can be found even there, although we have to search a bit because they are well guarded. We open the stable door and step into their world. Bales of straw, the muck cart in the corner, lead ropes in neon bright colors arranged in orderly rows on the wall. There we are in the narrow confines of a barn, the scent of horses engulfing us—and there they are, large, submissive creatures behind bars. That is the first encounter.

But it was not always like that. We human beings can be close to them these days, and yet horses are still very different from us. We have forgotten the path they traveled to be here—where they were put into stalls—and how that happened.

...the Horizon Was Wide

Horses are different. People know hardly anything about these animals that stand there in their stalls. They are alien creatures to us, as we are to them. Even if we have spent years with horses, on horses, among horses—even if we have a horse we call our own—the alienation remains. For the person who loves these creatures, who has loved them for his entire life, this sense of alienation is a constant stabbing ache. No matter how much knowledge about them he acquires, no matter how well he rides, no matter if he spurs his horse until "it" is raw and bleeding or the horse willingly carries him, he cannot get any more familiar, any more intimate. The horse does not become closer. He does not become trusting. With time, most people suppress this painful feeling that something is missing, or they become accustomed to it. They tell themselves that horses are just like that. Perhaps their yearning stays alive and they hope for a horse whisperer who will finally open the hearts of these creatures for them.

Horses are different. They do not allow themselves to be cracked open like a nut. A person who nevertheless does it against a horse's will may in fact be able to swallow the "seed" he has ripped from its shell, but the secret of the living growing "tree" will be forever hidden from him. If you want to learn to understand the nature of horses, you must approach them in a different way. If you want to have friendly conversations with them, you must meet them on an equal level. Only in that way will you be able to become part of their world, instead of coming as a conqueror, as one who wants to destroy. Of course we would gladly have the horse as a friend, but is there even a chance of that becoming a reality? Is it not more likely that what we call friendship with respect to horses is something our horse would call by a very different name, something he would much prefer to do without because this "friendship" always works to his detriment? Can there be a friendship when power is so unevenly distributed, when one "friend" keeps the other locked in a dungeon, when the whole world belongs to the one and the other cannot even call his body his own?

A person who seeks to master horses will always resort to instruments of force. But one who understands that he is a guest in the world of horses realizes he has neither the right nor a reason to punish a horse, or to fight with him. He does not issue commands, but rather makes an effort to learn something new with and from this animal, and to make his own presence as pleasant as possible. This basic politeness will change his behavior so radically that he will soon be accepted by horses without reservation.

It is not the stable door that opens the pathway to the realm of horses. Nor is it a particular method, of whatever kind, taught in clinics, seminars, or schools. Only the horses themselves can show us this path and teach us their language. We reach their world only when we have left behind any desire for control, claim to dominance, and arrogance of the mighty, and we open our eyes and our senses wide.

The world of horses is different. Horses today are forced to live in our human world and to subjugate themselves to rules and laws not their own. To us it is a foregone conclusion: stall and oats, saddle and tack, halter and bridle, all are necessary for their life. But horses are different. That difference begins in the way they perceive their surroundings and ends in their desire—actually a physical necessity—to be continually on the move. Horses live in movement. As mentioned, over millions of years their forebears adapted themselves to life on the endless steppes. From the tips of their ears to the bottoms of their hooves, horses are meant for a life in open grassland. They are specialists in wide open spaces, specialists in movement. Because of this, they see many things differently than humans who come from a much more circumscribed way of life.

Horses See Differently

Horses love the open. It gives them security. They like to see things from a great distance, and they can do that even better while grazing. Horses have panoramic vision—they can see nearly all around themselves, even with their heads down. It is only the area directly behind his body that a horse cannot see. Everything else is always in his view. But, because of the placement of his eyes on the side of his head, he can see only a very small slice of his surroundings in really sharp focus. He does see every movement, but he has less ability to focus than a human being. To clearly recognize and evaluate something, a horse must face whatever it is and raise his head. If you want to get a sense of how it is to see this way, experiment a bit with a wagging finger, or a pencil or something similar—seeing it only on the outer edge of your peripheral vision. You will notice whether something is there, and whether it moves, but you will not necessarily be able to immediately categorize and analyze it. This is how horses see at almost every point in their field of vision. If you do this little exercise with a partner, and hold your head rigid, you will be able to get a sense of the state of mind of a horse whose head and neck are not free but rather, are being restrained. You are practically forced to be in a continual state of fearful tension.

This is Toppur. He has been waiting for you. Toppur has kindly volunteered to guide you through this book. At his side, in the short sections that divide one chapter from the next, you can discover how things are in this other world. Take time for the journey. Set your thoughts free, and wander together over the great expanses...

The World of Horses

If you observe horses closely, you will discover how very much of their being together is defined by harmony and play. Our guide Toppur is "accosted" on his way here to us. The young bay stallion playfully attacks him—he is excited because they have all just come to this new pasture. What looks at first glance like a fight is harmless play. You can see this clearly in the relaxed expression of both horses: happily extended upper lips, mobile ears and nostrils, very relaxed posture.

Toppur lets the "challenges" of the weaker provocateur play themselves out. He has more important things to do at the moment and has discovered something in the distance. Even though Shannon is disturbing him in the performance of his duties, and even enthusiastically bites him, this lead stallion does not lose his composure. He accepts the playful attack in the spirit of fun. Horses are just different!

"This feels really good!" Horses love to roll in mud, sand, and dust. There he lies like a fat beetle, all fours stretched in the air. This is Max, most happily wallowing. He is enjoying scratching his back on the ground, and his upper lip is stretched in pleasure, similar to the lips of the playing stallions seen on pages 20 and 21. Can you see it? What a joyful life—do you happen to have an itch right now?

Horses Live Differently

Horses are constantly in motion. They love vast expanses of space. Horses do not reside anywhere in particular, they do not seek permanent housing—they travel around. Horses would rather be outside under the open sky where they have endless space, than protected in a locked room. Whereas we human beings hide ourselves, horses seek wide open spaces. An area of a size that we can comfortably oversee is menacingly small for them. For horses, security is not a roof overhead or a warm cave, but rather, the open air, free space, community, the closeness of the others. Their home is the herd. Horses sleep or doze, but someone is always keeping watch. Horses are very social creatures. A horse alone is insecure, uneasy, and unhappy.

Horses Pass Time Differently

A free horse in nature spends most of his time procuring nourishment. He is always busy eating. And that is how it should be because a horse gets the energy for life from the uptake of a quantity of nutrients constantly passing through a very long digestive tract, not from a supply in concentrated form like we human beings. Compared to a horse, we dine on "calorie bombs."

The horse eats grass. As a pasture animal he has become specially adapted to a food that provides relatively little energy. That is why he needs large quantities of it. And he lives on the constant flow of voluminous amounts of food. He cannot store food the way ruminants do. Any blockage in the digestive tract can be deadly—impaction colic! In this respect he is very delicate. His digestion must be constantly active. The flow is not reversible—horses cannot vomit.

Eating continually, digesting thoroughly. Horses do not occupy themselves in quest of a big "meal." They graze and saunter around, here a little grass, there a little grass, then a visit with a buddy, some scratching, dozing, eating again...Although they eat nearly all the time and everywhere, in doing so they are not goal-oriented. The "hunting" instinct is lacking. Complicated procurement of food or preparing for future needs is not their thing. After all, something is always growing somewhere.

Horses Interact Differently

Because of their social nature, horses are emotionally susceptible. They adopt each other's moods. It is as though a current flows back and forth among the animals. If one lifts a head because he has seen something, the rest of the herd will quickly do that too. And they will all look excitedly in the same direction. Horses love harmony among themselves—for the most part they alternate attuning to one another. They scratch each other, with their teeth, in the same rhythm, in the same spot. They trot and canter in unison, and they wrestle the same way. Horses like to feel at one with their friends—they organize themselves around mutual harmony.

Yet, this harmony can be disrupted. Horses in captivity are often aggressive toward one another and can develop strong, rigid herd hierarchies. Such "pecking" order is, to be sure, a symptom of stress that comes from a restricted way of life determined by strangers. Under natural circumstances there is hardly anything to fight about—each can go his own separate way. The sometimes harsh quality of interaction among domestic horses is "normal" behavior for these animals only in the sense that the asocial offspring of certain zoo inhabitants are "normal." One experiences this too with human beings who, unwillingly locked up together in close quarters, must interact with one another. The more space horses have and the more it is possible for them to organize themselves in their own fashion, the more harmonious their life together will be.

Horses Perceive Differently

Not only are horses able to instantaneously pick up the mood of others, they also are able to read the disposition of other animals almost as though they could read their thoughts. This is a very useful ability when you travel among many predators every day. The striped cousins of our horses amazed their human observers with surprising behavior: on some days, these zebras would flee as soon as they merely caught sight of a lion; on others, they continued their relaxed grazing while their deadly enemy slinked past them. Apparently, the zebras knew exactly when a lion was satiated and lazy, or was moving only because he was thirsty. On these occasions, they were not afraid of him. They interpreted his moods and behaved accordingly. And the zebras had still more information about the lions, the origins of which remained a puzzle to the scientists. On the big cat's hunting days, the zebras knew exactly what the lion's plans were. It was only when the lion actually became active that the scientists could see if it would be a gnu day, or a zebra day. The zebras, however, seemed to know immediately—as though they had read it in the lion's mind.

Horses are often better informed about a person's feelings and intentions than the person himself. A well-known and relevant example is the horse that refuses to jump because he knows that his rider does not actually trust himself to make it. The horse refuses even though the rider violently tries to force him. The rider perceives only his own conscious intention to jump. The horse perceives his unconscious reluctance. Only when the rider has "thrown his heart over" the obstacle, will the horse jump after it. The many horses who shy at a particular spot because their rider expects them to shy there are also demonstrating this quality. Then, on another day, there is a different rider in the saddle who is completely unaware of the "trouble" spot and suddenly, a miracle happens: the "fear" is gone and the horse, without hesitation, moves past the problem area.

The Fleeing Horse

Horses also move differently than we do. Movement assumes such a central place in their lives that we will delve very comprehensively into this subject. Horses are creatures of movement: running animals, or flight animals, as we like to say. But is this description truly accurate? Certainly horses that are very much involved with human beings are frequently startled and often try to flee mindlessly. But, have you ever seen horses in bitter conflict? Or watched one chase away a dog? Horses are dangerous opponents when they decide to fight.

The regal behavior of equids living in the wild, not to mention the inquisitive spirit that the occasional lively offspring of our domesticated horses still frequently display, even today, leads to the conjecture that we ourselves, through our methods of breeding, keeping, and training, have "infected" horses with the tendency to flight. Actually, foals seem to find everything new exciting. If they are startled they come back to investigate the unknown as though magically drawn to it. Horses are powerful animals that can drive respect into a full grown bull and smash the skull of an attacking dog. Horses display blind panic—the panic of the steppes—only when their world goes up in flames, as during a prairie fire, for example. We see our horses as frightened animals prone to flight, but often it is we humans who have laid the foundation for this behavior by the totally unnatural way we keep and interact with them. Could it not be that the loss of their own world has made our horses so easily startled and fearful?

Winning a Horse's Friendship

How can I, a human being, become close with horses? How can I establish a dialog between us? What must I do so that horses understand me? What must I learn so that I understand them?

Horses come to an understanding among themselves in a language that, for the most part, is hidden from our senses. They have their own culture and their own kind of knowledge. But the different worlds of horses and human beings have not co-existed in equality for a very long time. We human beings are everywhere, our world has become all-encompassing, and a horse these days can live only within it. We have taken horses out of their world and the way of life for which they evolved for millions of years. We brought them into our human world that is so alien and cold that even we sometimes become afraid. We hold all the power and at the same time are fleeing from it. We come to horses in search of a world that is older, more whole and integrated than the one we have created. But we do not find it. And we do not come with open hands. We want to experience connectedness and harmony, yet we bring war, despotism, and disruption. We dream of transformation and new paths, yet our actions manifest as dominance and control. We want to find freedom, but we take it away from horses with every single step. To horses such actions are incomprehensible and oppressive.

Changes in the Worlds

The world of horses—that expansive, free world of the steppes, the endless pace through which the herd wanders—is forever lost. The unique world of horses now exists only internally—it is preserved within each individual horse. But even in his "inner" world the horse is no longer safe. These days we want horses to give us not only their body, but their spirit as well and we oppress them more and more.

The person who understands that he, as a human being, has all the power and that there is none left over for the horse, has reached a turning point in his relationship to the animal. He suddenly feels very different needs and desires with respect to these creatures. He begins to pull himself back a bit and gives the horses more space. He begins to adapt himself to them and learn about them. And he starts to become open to their completely different point of view and in doing so, he gives their world a new reality.

Having a dialog with horses necessitates acquiring a brand new view of things. It means perceiving horses differently. It means being on their side. How does what I am doing feel to my horse? How does he feel when I am doing it? What could I do to make things easier for him, to make him feel better? This point of view can completely transform our relationship with one another—but it is not easy to maintain. It is very likely that you will go off course if you do not continually get feedback from your horse. Often it is simply easier

Horses love to play in water. At one time, a swimming pond for horses was part of every village. Horses find great pleasure in bathing—just like young Shane here.

Out Walking Together

Here comes Toppur, and I am accompanying him. The two of us are walking very matter-of-factly beside one another, neither crowding the other. Person and horse, side by side, make a lovely picture full of harmony as we approach. As we come closer, something interesting becomes noticeable—there is a subtle dialog back and forth between us.

In the first photo, Toppur and I are traveling in a relaxed walk. Then the stallion becomes aware of horses on the horizon. Toppur accelerates and moves into a trot. What he has seen interests him and he would like to have a closer look, perhaps there are some mares among them. He moves faster and faster, his body becomes taut. In a moment he will whinny and race off. But Toppur stays. He slows down again and quietly walks on. Why did that happen? What did I do? What signal persuaded him to control himself? All that can be seen is a soft glance to the side, no "stop" signal, no command that the horse is expected to obey.

not to question yourself, or to hear your horse's answer. But, on the path to his world and friendship, you must orient yourself to him and keep him constantly in your focus. In this, the critical thing is an awakened eye.

The Circular Flow of Communication

It is hard to believe that something as ineffable as a person's inner state can have any influence on a massive horse. And yet, there is nothing mysterious about it. You do not need to possess the evil eye or magical super powers. But then, what is it that makes horses react the way they do? Look once more at the photo sequence on pages 26 and 27 with the Icelandic stallion, Toppur. As the horse trots off, I run with him. I keep the same pace and rhythm, though my body tension is somewhat different than his—it's looser, softer, and concentrated on the process of running. I share the movement with the stallion, but I do not share his excitement, the excitement that is pressuring him out of our harmonious togetherness. Then Toppur, for his part, begins to share with me: in the fourth photo you can see how his outward-directed energy begins to come back to us, how his tension recedes from its peak. We are both focusing our senses in the same direction, into Toppur's body. Where is the center? Where is the weight carried? At that point, Toppur slows the pace and rhythm and comes back to himself. The circle of our conversation is now closed again. In the last photo, Toppur is back with me on our common path. His hindquarters came off the track a bit as he increased his pace. Now he is moving straight as an arrow again, his gaze attentively ahead.

Togetherness is the basis for understanding between horses who wish each other well. They share feelings and adapt themselves to one another. Something a single horse notices can move the whole herd. Our relationship with a horse begins when we achieve this feeling-based connection and take the horse's point of view. We ask him: "How do you feel about this?"

A New Perspective

Reflecting, observing, sensing—those are the tasks for human beings. A person who begins to see the world through the eyes of his horse becomes that horse's kindred spirit. And suddenly, completely new forms of communication are possible. Now external signals are of lesser importance. We understand each other directly, instantaneously, because the sharing of feelings creates an interface, an entranceway into the other's world.

Togetherness is the foundation from which everything else proceeds. Togetherness—not hierarchy—puts us on the same level. Togetherness is the prerequisite for influencing each other from within the depths of our being. And that relates to feelings and movement—horse and person on one wavelength in a dialog of movement. As with musicians,

"We are creatures of movement..." Running, jostling, romping, tussling, these boys are enthusiastically getting to know their new terrain together. Often it is like a schoolyard at recess. Once again you can see the typical "play" expressions on the horses' faces.

in the beginning there is a search for the common key and rhythm: before they begin to play a piece, musicians attune to one another. Togetherness and sharing openly are the first and oldest form of understanding.This is the archetype of every meaningful communication. Being together in harmony means shared feelings with one another. I share yours—I share mine.

Instead of enlarging the chasm between the world of horses and the world of human beings, we can connect these two worlds so that each influences the other, transforming and strengthening it. What this means and where it leads us is something we shall now discover—together with the horses!

Listening, observing, sharing feelings—these are not just techniques but rather genuinely empathetic points of view that reach horses and win their trust. While Toppur enjoys the surroundings and our outing in his own way, we will proceed to the next chapter and lay the foundation for our relationship. Here is where it all begins—in the freedom of open space.

"The only true voyage of discovery consists not in seeking new lands, but rather in seeing with new eyes."

~Marcel Proust

AS FAR AS OUR HOOVES WILL CARRY US—Free, Open Space

A Mute Animal

My dog yelps when I step on his paw. "Oh dear, you poor thing. I did not mean to do that! I'm sorry, I did not see you." My cat meows when there is something I am supposed to do for him. "Okay. Just a moment and I'll get the door for you." You don't hear anything from a horse in similar situations. Horses say nothing in this way. They remain silent. Although horses lead a very expressive social life, they rarely communicate with sound. Even their language stems from the wide open spaces of the steppes, from the life of scattered grazing herds, and it suits the horse's wide angle of vision. The language of horses orients itself to seeing. It becomes understandable through the sense of sight.

Horse language in view

Understanding between human beings is concentrated in a different sense—for us, hearing plays the major role. On the whole, we surely take in most information with our eyes and seeing is the first and most prominent sense with which we investigate our surroundings. Yet, the ear is our organ for person-to-person communication. It is here that we have our social "feel" and our sense for false notes. A nuance can reveal exactly how our partner in conversation means what he is saying, and we hear the subtle difference in his voice. We register facts with our sense of sight: "That I would like to see!" The sense of sight "oversees" and checks impressions from the other senses. It "watches" over the situation, and "keeps an eye" on everything. Our sense of sight has a close connection to our rational awareness. On the other hand, it is through our ears that someone speaks to our feelings. It is in what we hear that our social consciousness resides. A sound, a certain tone, can instantly awaken sleeping emotions, it is a favorite way to access the human unconscious—film scores or marching music are examples of this. Even department store "muzak" is intended to access this not-entirely-rational back door to our feelings. A person's mood can be very strongly influenced by what is heard. A piece of music can bring us to the verge of tears. Memories suddenly come alive and stir the emotions.

The whole herd had just been galloping, happily excited, through the high grass. Now they have all begun grazing—snorting, the rhythmical sound of grass being eaten, a scent of herbs in the air. The Haflinger Kim, too, is deeply engrossed in his meal. A woman arrives in the meadow. She wants to work with Kim.

Acoustic (aural) stimuli influence a person's impressions much more directly than visual ones. And we can easily ignore visual stimuli—eyes closed and it is over! Unpleasant sounds continue to disturb our sensitive, harmony-requiring ears, but we soon become accustomed to an unlovely sight. We look past it and do not allow ourselves to be moved by it. The eye presorts things. Could this be why visual art, art that reaches people via the eyes, has a far more difficult time reaching its public than music? Is it because our sense of sight is unstable in the midst of the flood of visual information, quickly turned off, and likes to remain distanced and superficial?

Horses Whisper Differently

The social sense

Vocalizing is the typical human form of communication. Horses prefer visual "language." Where we are content to make telephone calls, they prefer television. In many instances, we find the ear sufficient for social understanding. For us, there is a very strong connection to other human beings in hearing them. For humans, a sense of belonging is primarily shaped by sound, by the tone. Whether it is technically specific language relating to a given topic, or a particular dialect, human herd members recognize one another primarily by sound patterns. Someone who is deaf or hard of hearing, therefore, has far more problems feeling as though he belongs than someone who sees badly or not at all. A pleasant social atmosphere for us is synonymous with harmony, resonance, a good tone, and no false notes. All of these perceptions are grounded in sound. Being a good listener, giving someone a "hearing" and "lending an ear" all have a strong social component.

Of course, we have other forms of communication besides those that are centered on sound. There are many visual signals to which we respond every day—from the blinking light on an answering machine to the gestures of someone directing traffic. Horses, too, whinny to one another and can take up contact that way. And after a while with us, they learn to follow our vocal signals the way a driver learns to stop at a red light. However, on this level of communication the element of social connection is not very significant. Certainly we can direct a horse with vocal commands—be they shouted or whispered: "Halt!" "Forward!" or even, "Turn around!" And if the person speaking the orders has mastered his subject, everything will function well and proceed as things do at a busy intersection with good traffic signals. However, leaving aside the braking and accelerating, there is no conversation going on, the person is not actually getting an answer from his horse. A dialog is out of the question at this socially atypical level of communication, because horses whisper differently. If we cause insane chaos, horses will not vocalize their opinions or protest by making sounds. Even when in terrible pain, a horse does not scream or whimper. That is why a human observer is perhaps not able to recognize a horse's suffering—he cannot "hear" it. A horse remains mute, he does not "speak up" because he communicates on a totally different level.

"Listening" with the eyes—different levels of the senses

If we want to form a relationship with a horse, we should not wait until he opens his mouth and begins to utter words like Balaam's donkey in the Bible (Numbers 22:2–25:9): Because he was in a hurry and intent on achieving his own agenda, Balaam did not see the angel blocking his path. Balaam's donkey, however, did see the messenger of God, and refused to run over him, despite Balaam's attempts to force her onward. By her refusal to obey her unseeing human master, the donkey was saving Balaam's life. Balaam, however, noticed only his clairvoyant donkey's disobedience—and beat her for it. After the third beating, God gave the donkey the power of speech so that the mistreated animal could "reason" with her master. It is then revealed that, had the donkey succumbed to the beatings and followed her master's instructions, Balaam—and only Balaam—would have been dead.

The "talking" donkey in the Bible

When we honor the unique level of understanding that horses have, we begin to "hear" with our eyes. Then, perhaps, we can achieve insight and begin to carry on a conversation with our horses, without heavenly intervention.

Room for Free Expression

A person who wants to communicate with horses needs a horse that will speak to him. And a person who wants to learn a little something about horses needs a horse that freely expresses himself. For a dialog to exist and so that the horse can truly be "heard" by us, he must have an opportunity to answer in his own way: at the very least, with agreement or refusal.

Horses share their feelings with us in silence, in that they go away and evade, or they come and seek our company. If a horse's declaration is to become visible, we must absolutely allow him the opportunity to express himself in his own way. A person who is truly interested in a dialog will not tie him up, restrain or confine him. How can a horse possibly speak in such circumstances? The greater the space a horse has to call "his own" the less likely it is that his answer will be misunderstood. If he runs away, terrified, as soon as you appear on the scene, then that is a very clear message, which unfortunately, shatters

Horses speak by moving

Kim Comes

He is contentedly grazing in his pasture when this woman comes. She has a whip, halter, and rope with her, which means that she would like to work with Kim. She greets the gelding and puts the halter on, so that he knows for certain what her intentions are. Then she sets him free, walks a few steps away, and asks him if he would like to come along. Kim would like to. He leaves his meal of lush grass and strides along with her toward the pasture gate. He is proud and free beside the woman—he does not follow like a subjugated creature. Kim goes with Kirsten because he wants to work. He understood her offer and gladly accepted it.

Here, the person very distinctly gives the horse free space. She asks. In the photos you can see how Kim responds to this freedom—namely, in the affirmative. But, there is more. As they are walking Kim suddenly discovers that they are both being observed from a distance, that someone is "shooting" them with focused gaze. It is Bernd, the photographer. "Hey, there is someone staring at us!" Kirsten senses Kim's concern and responds the way a horse would—she looks in the same direction. "Ah, yes—that's okay. I know him." That could well be the translation of the message Kirsten conveys to Kim. She does not need to tell him that, it simply comes across that way because the two of them are on the same wavelength. "Okay, there is nothing to worry about," and calmed, the gelding trots with Kirsten up the hill toward the gate out of the meadow.

any illusion that he finds you and your requests or demands good in any way whatsoever. First and foremost it is free space, plenty of room to move, that makes a horse's free expression possible. A person who denies a horse this suppresses a clear answer, silences his horse, and deprives himself of information.

The Necessary Distance

How long has it been since you closely studied the facial features of a person near and dear to you—the shade of the eyebrows, the shape of nose and eyes, the angle of the mouth, the fine downy hair on the cheeks, and how the face changes when this person is thoughtful, injured, surprised, happy or relaxed?

Sufficient space—room to see

The first step in communicating with a horse is "listening" to him by opening your eyes, seeing with a calm, receptive, unbiased gaze. This conscious, considerate, and "listening" way of seeing is seldom achieved these days. In fact, it is hardly ever practiced anymore.

Today we live in a visual society and the eye dominates all the other senses. We only believe what we can see. Our eyes are constantly busy verifying, sorting, checking, cataloging. Our surroundings generally do not permit us even the occasional relaxed, sweeping glance into the distance. A far-seeing, wide-open view is something we can still occasionally enjoy by the ocean or in the mountains, but otherwise the eye is held captive by written characters, computer monitors, TV screens, the walls of our homes and offices, and skyscraper canyons.

And horses, too, are captive. Human beings are always very close by. For a person, with his comparatively narrow field of vision to be able to see the entire horse, he must be a good four steps away. A typical box stall is too small for that. Larger areas make it possible for us to have a more comprehensive perception, while at the same time, giving the horse more room to express himself. No wonder that so many horses and human beings no longer understand one another these days—they are in too small a space, there is simply not enough room.

The Language of Horses

- *Running off, fleeing, and turning away always mean: NO!*
- *Tensing, stiffening, contracting, wide-open eyes always mean: FEAR!*
- *Enthusiastic romping, playing, taking pleasure in movement (almost) always mean: JOY!*
- *Coming to you, not leaving your side, seeking interaction with you (nearly) always mean: YES!*

Humans and horses both lack free space

In Harmony with the Horse

At the beginning of this chapter a horse is standing in the midst of a field of grass: it is Kim. Kirsten asks him if he wants to come along to the arena—and his answer is clearly "yes." How is it that this horse behaves like this—readily, willingly leaving his large green pasture for the confined space of the arena, the effort of work? Why is this horse so motivated? To get the answers, you must be patient a bit longer. In the course of our time together, things will become clearer, and maybe you will soon come up with several

Free space as the basis for togetherness

answers on your own. First, though, let's get back to the situation at hand—back to Kim.

What would have happened had Kim turned away, if he had signaled, "No, thank you?" What would Kirsten do? She would, one more time, clearly invite him to join her, perhaps also letting him know that it meant a lot to her. But, what if Kim still did not want to come, if he had even walked away? Kirsten would respect his position, take away the halter, say her goodbyes with a treat, and leave him in his pasture because his hunger is greater than his desire to join her.

A horse's desires should count just as much as ours do, at least if we are talking about partnership and friendship. I do not enjoy feeling like an overseer of slaves when with my horses. There can be no genuine unity if I must coerce them. Let's turn the question around: would you have fun if you were forcefully dragged into doing something? Why should I even consider applying this pressure to my horse or myself? These days, no one and nothing demands that we must ride. Instead of forcing my horse, I will sit in the grass and play with my dog, or think of something else to do.

Freedom, As We Mean It...

Horses galloping on the horizon, manes waving, a rider illuminated by the evening light... freedom and expanses of space are what horses symbolize to us, whether they are wild or tamed. Man dreams of himself on horseback, leaving everything behind and riding off into the setting sun.

The song of freedom

Freedom: this word awakens many feelings because we know how it is not supposed to be—dependent, tied up, locked in. Every one of us has had, at least once, the experience of being "harnessed" for a purpose imposed on us, being ordered about, pressed or driven. Such a situation is disheartening, and over time will diminish the life force. If you are constantly at the mercy of such circumstances you begin to feel ever more helpless, weak, trapped. Freedom promises an end to all this. It is over. Coercion has been left behind. He who is free can refuse anything and everything asked of him, if he wants to. He decides what he will and will not do because he is master of himself.

Horses feel differently

The fact that someone is walking around unrestricted by tight clothing—or even completely in the nude—does not necessarily mean that he feels free, or that he is enjoying himself. He might, in fact, feel exposed and vulnerable. Or perhaps someone dreams of clamping a snug-fitting helmet on his head and being strapped into the bucket seat of a race car so that he can go whizzing down an asphalt track between guard rails at high speed. That would be freedom as this person understands it. We do not discover this until we have a conversation with him. And what about riding? It could well be that another person feels free as the proverbial American Indian who galloped bareback on his horse. But what about the horse whose neck he clung to—the horse that had to carry him off? Did the horse share that feeling of freedom?

What Does My Horse Dream Of?

The thrill of riding happens on the back of a horse but it would be naïve to believe that the horse feels the same as we do. He experiences our joy from an entirely different perspective: from the bottom. This changes things.

Good feelings under saddle?

Can I equate freedom for my horse with the mere fact that he no longer wears a saddle or bridle? Or, does this "nakedness" only fulfill a human being's dream of freedom, a dream that has very little to do with a horse's perception? Freedom is, above all, a feeling, and that is why the subject is so difficult. This feeling can be created by external things,

but whether or not one actually feels free because of them depends absolutely on whether, or how, one actually sees these things or can perceive them. It is only because of perception that the sought-after feeling—to be free in this moment—is connected with certain external circumstances. How good does my horse feel when I feel good sitting on top of him? We must carefully distinguish between our own thinking and the very individual perception of the horse in question.

Freedom—this feeling comes from within and so can hardly be identified or defined by external trappings. A halter or a bridle can mean to my horse, "Oh no! I'm going to be annoyed again," or "Great! Now we'll finally get going! I've waited all day for you!" We must know how our horse feels and how he sees a situation or thing before we can characterize him as "free." How does he feel as he is doing whatever-it-is? Does he have a choice, a genuine alternative? Can he refuse to do it if he does not want to? Is there a way out for him? Can he find it? Can he say "no" and feel absolutely certain that his refusal will be acknowledged and respected? Or, has his spirit been broken so badly that he now believes his two-legged "master" is all-powerful and resistance is futile? One who no longer believes in freedom will not run away, even in an endless prairie: there is no point to it anymore, so, head hanging low, he remains where he is.

A free horse?

Carefree Vagabonds

A vast expanse of wide open space—that is the natural home of horses. For thousands of years these animals lived as wanderers on the wide open steppes in Asia. When I want to keep my horse in a manner suited to his nature, I must make sure that he has plenty of space and room to move around. If my horse has a lot of acres to roam, open stalls, varied terrain, and the company of other horses, he continually has the opportunity to make choices for himself and act accordingly. Being in a box stall only gives him an opportunity to choose whether to turn his head or his hindquarters toward the barn aisle. The horse that has to make his own decisions every day keeps mentally more fit: he has to decide whether he wants to be inside or out; whether to go to the water trough and have a drink; whether he wants to climb the hill and enjoy the view alone up there or stay near the other horses; whether he wants to go for a dip in the pond, eat blackberry leaves, lazily slouch around, go for a gallop and play, or simply stand there and doze...

Everyday freedom

Keeping a horse in accordance with his nature absolutely improves his well-being. But, it is not only how we keep a horse that affords us a chance to give him more freedom. Even our daily interaction with him offers many opportunities to give him some "space." I can use a longer lead rope to lead my horse, and I can also allow him to lead me once in a while. I can adapt myself to his wishes for a change rather than just pulling him along behind me or constantly correcting him. I can, whenever possible, let him run free, be

at liberty, leave him untied when I groom or tack up. What's that you say? He is running away? No, he is not badly trained or spoiled. He just shared his feelings with me; he gave me some information. He was simply telling me, "I do not like that, please stop it!"

I can now go after him, bring him back, and in the traditional manner, continue what I was going to do: "You must do this!" I would be "master" again, and my horse would have to endure whatever it was I had in mind to do. That would be that, as far as freedom is concerned, and I would have my peace...so much for the dream. Or, I could go after him, offer him a piece of my delicious apple and profusely, sincerely apologize for my tactless conduct. "I am sorry. I was clumsy and did not listen well. Please excuse me. Can we still speak with one another again?" At any rate, that is how I would begin my apology.

I will take my space for myself—El Paso lives! A person has to capture his interest and win him over, because this horse does not surrender his freedom so easily.

A Genuine Alternative

Free space is what creates the possibility for a true dialog. The horse can leave or he can come, he can say "yes" or "no." We want the horse to sense his freedom, to feel it, to realize it. This is how Kirsten brings Kim, her Haflinger, from the pasture: "Do you want to come, or not?" she asks. The horse may, should, and must be able to decide for himself, because it is only from a freely made decision that our very special kind of relationship can grow. We want to share pride, joy, and time together with the horse, not force ourselves on him. That can only happen if the horse is with us of his own free will. For freedom to even be possible there must be several options available, among which free choice is permitted. In addition to the option of coming along the horse can walk away, keep his distance, do something else. And he must know that he has this freedom and can use it at any time.

Freedom to choose

"Yes" or "no" translated into the language of open space is to approach or take flight. In open, free space the horse speaks a visible language that every human being can understand. In such free space the person can learn to refine his skills of observation to such a degree that he begins to sense his horse's feelings. That ability makes him independent of academic theories or clichés of conventional wisdom that perhaps do not even suit his individual horse at all. Instead of being informed by opinions or contradictory advice, he now experiences directly and first hand the needs and preferences of this one unique horse. This horse protests when he is over-faced, discusses things that do not make sense, and rejoices when he does something exactly right—understanding!

Freedom in learning

El Paso and His Song of Freedom

He looks so harmless—a small, pale pinto, not very powerfully built, a crossbred. But El Paso is an unyielding animal. He does not let himself be ruled by human beings, not even when they use violent force. The person who tries, winds up biting down on granite.

This delicate little horse proves to be a tough fighter whom no one has yet been able to force to surrender.

No one knows exactly how El Paso came by this toughness. It may have happened in his youth, because he is like this, not only with human beings, but with other horses when they get aggressive and he cannot escape. El Paso grew up as the playmate of a stallion a little bit older than he. The little pinto was bought as a companion, so he became a playmate, or, rather, a "plaything," because in the small paddock where the horses were confined, he was subjected to the attacks of the bigger and stronger bully day after day. In his young years, El Paso had to swallow a lot and hold it inside. While doing that he likely learned quite a bit—how one deflects tyranny and aggression by becoming unyielding, demonstrating that one can "tough it out" and if necessary, breaking through the fence. "Surrendering and submitting brings nothing! Life is merciless!" That became his motto. The only sensible answer to force is to leave, or "hang tough" and take it. El Paso does not let himself be held back, even with chains he tears loose and runs over people if he has to. But this gelding is in no way vicious. On the contrary, he is a fundamentally decent fellow who never starts a fight. But, this horse is capable of powerful resistance when someone tries to "ride roughshod" over him. He will not yield one hoof's length and does not let himself be intimidated. We human beings are not accustomed to that sort of behavior from horses.

El Paso fights for his freedom and physical safety—no more and no less. Of course, he is not invincible. Like every living thing he has a weak spot. It is in his balance, so necessary for a creature of movement like the horse. A horse has his fear point on his back—in precisely the spot where a person sits when he rides. The methods of conventional training would have been to eventually overcome El Paso's resistance, to "break" him. By riding him, a person can very effectively bring a horse out of balance, mercilessly pounding on his back with each stride, day after day, sitting on his neck, driving him to total exhaustion, and taking possession of his body in the literal sense of the word.

El Paso was lucky. No one attempted to break his stubborn nature because in this horse's life, there is a second weak point: Astrid, his owner! She loves him. And she could never have stood by and watched as someone "broke" El Paso. Astrid stayed true to her little pinto, even though everyone advised her to rid herself of this useless "thing" as quickly as possible. She made a fool of herself with him everywhere. Tough guys like him have no sense of devoted gratitude. What for? Now El Paso not only has an uncommon character, he also has an uncommon coat color that is obvious even from a distance. So Astrid continually encountered pitying and scornful comments, "No, you do not really still have him, do you? He is only good for meat," even when El Paso was just standing peacefully nearby. But Astrid adapted herself to him rather than demanding that he adjust to her. It would not work any other way. She learned to play with El Paso, or rather, he played with her and she did her best to play along with his games. Sometimes it was difficult. He was so unreachable. Oh well, at least he seemed to amuse himself with her every once in awhile.

Today El Paso is a reliable trail horse exactly like the one Astrid had always wanted. The two of them have covered many, many miles together. But last summer there was no vacation riding trip because Astrid was injured. Not El Paso but another horse had trampled her leg. Because of her injury she could only come to visit infrequently and El Paso was worried then. This stoic, unshakeable horse suddenly showed very strong feelings. El Paso was overjoyed when Astrid arrived. He put on a spectacular show when she watched him work. He seemed to grow wings in order to do a passage—a movement too advanced for his level of training. And the first time Astrid was again able to sit on him, El Paso carried her as though he were walking on clouds.

El Paso is a rebel and will always be one. He has to be won over to whatever it is one

A free, willing, "yes" to the work that will soon take place—Kim and Kirsten as they leave the pasture.

wants to do with him. He is not "obedient" in the typical sense. But, he wants to please his Astrid, stay with her, and he knows that she only initiates things that are interesting, relaxing, and useful to him. That is why he lets himself be influenced by her. That is why he listens to her.

Between Argument and Handshake

Conversations while walking

Free space creates the basis for an entirely new relationship between man and horse. Instead of being trapped in the narrow boundaries of one-way "cue" language, person and horse conduct a many-faceted conversation with one another. Movement is of central significance here—it is the subject and the medium of conversation, of the language, as we will come to see. Horses come to understanding in movement; movement is their "speech." And we will converse with them about movement as follows: we will walk and run along with them.

Do as I tell you!

Human conversation with a horse is usually reduced to a language of commands. The person gives the orders that the horse must obey. The flow of communication is from top to bottom. The horse always remains passive. He receives the person's requests and carries them out—or not. His only "room to maneuver" is between obeying and not obeying.

Of course, this limit on communication is not necessary if we expand our concept of language. The disadvantage of the spoken word is that only one "track" is possible, otherwise there is a cacophony of voices and no one understands anything. When there is no exchange, spoken language leads to imbalance in a relationship. Whoever has the words has the power. The horse has no words, so he has no opportunity to be heard; he always remains the mute servant. There is great power in monopoly of speech. It can only be balanced by taking turns speaking. Otherwise the other, the one who is supposed only to be hearing (and obeying) is driven off by the flood of words.

The Rules of Spatial Language

A free, lively dialog between a person and a horse requires the following:

***Asking:** we ask the horse and take his suggestions.*

***Offering a genuine choice:** the horse can freely and independently choose from several alternatives.*

***Accepting:** we accept our horse's answer and adapt ourselves accordingly.*

Maybe it is the either/or nature of our spoken language that facilitates a hierarchical relationship with animals. Although even human beings can experience wordless understanding and communication through touch and body language, we apparently lack awareness of the potential of this spontaneous communication by which information can be simultaneously transmitted and received in many directions. That opens up a completely new dimension of understanding with one another. Side-by-side and simultaneous exchange are the rule. Because we understand one another, a glance is enough. But apparently many human beings lack the experience of parity in relationship and even the imagination to visualize such a thing. A hierarchy-free language means "room to maneuver" for both person and horse.

The dictate of spoken language.

Even the horses in this book live in a tightly restricted, cultivated landscape. They can no longer wander wherever they choose. During a walk with Toppur I get in his way—on purpose. The photos show two different scenarios. In the first one, I stop Toppur softly and fluidly with clear body language. I do it carefully for the purpose of demonstration. How does he respond to me and how does he feel as he does it? Study the horse's expression and let the overall impression have its effect.

Multisensory Perception

Perhaps you very much enjoy talking to your horse. I do not in any way want to talk you out of doing that. On the contrary, somehow the horses always get our message when we speak to them with genuine feeling. But as just explained the danger with speech is its one-track nature. This method of communication is a marathon monologue in which the horse has no chance to have his say: either we talk ourselves into something in which the horse is relegated to the role of a mute doll, or we slip, perhaps without wanting to, into a command hierarchy. Playing such a passive role is, understandably, not very motivating for the horse. He is not asked his opinion, no one listens to him, his voice does not count. A person who wants to be a good listener must expand his field of vision and make himself more "fluent" on the visual level, the horse's level. He will become open and receptive, as well as instantaneously responsive, to the horse's communication. It is possible to practice

seeing as empathetically as one listens in an intimate conversation. Learn to "see" the subtle "tones," hear what is unsaid. School your eye the way a musician trains his ear. Harmonious communication on this visual level is comparable to many voices singing together—a synchronized interplay, a vocal group into which each blends his voice and yet remains himself. And it is precisely the blending of many voices that lets a much more interesting, brand new entirety come to be.

To see the melody of movement and to get a sense for the music of horses we must "come down off our high horse"—literally—and work with our horse on the ground. Such perception will not develop when a person unknowingly fiddles around incorrectly for years on the horse's back. With a rider on top, it is not possible for the horse to use the corrective of distancing himself. His space for "speech" is reduced to bolting, or bucking off the intolerable presence. The greater the horse's freedom to communicate, the better, the safer the feedback, and its more pleasurable for all concerned. Begin by training your eye for this wordless and silent communication, for this language of movement in open space. Try to perceive the horse's moods.

The manner in which we look at something is a form of communication. Perhaps you have experienced an unusual sensation behind you, the feeling that something is there, and when you involuntarily turned around, someone is indeed staring at you. We can, sometimes, involuntarily sense more intense looks. Horses have a very highly developed sensitivity in this respect. That is how Kim noticed that someone was watching the two of them. What is more interesting, though, is how the photo series on page 33 continued. Even though Kim was immediately behind her, Kirsten sensed his slightly disquieted glance. As though she were a horse, she felt his uneasiness and responded by communicating in the same way: with a wider angled gaze she encompassed her horse, the reason for his uneasiness, and the person causing it. This "It's okay, I'm keeping my eye on it," is a very horse-like response. A lead herd member would also respond that way. Because the person and the horse are communicating on the same level, a glance can become a message. Kirsten does not need to calm Kim or call him back to attention, for here, in open space, an inner exchange can take place, one that requires no

The art of listening

Now to the second scenario: this looks totally different! Toppur has just had the idea that it would be great fun to tear off into the valley. I however cannot go along with him because I know that after a few leaps he is going to be much too fast and too far ahead of me. So, before he actually gets started I move energetically into his path and try to stop him. I block his movement much more aggressively than in the last scene, yet Toppur apparently takes it more positively. He is even displaying his "let's play" expression. Why? Read "Toppur's Answer," on page 42, and "Balance in Communication" on page 52. There you will see how we proceed from this situation and how Toppur reinstates the communicative balance between us.

The art of feeling

The art of observing

"'We will just threaten him a little bit, with one finger!' he said, as he placed it on the trigger."

~Stanislaw J. Lec

explicit signals because the two of them are on one wavelength! Kirsten neither actively leads (Come on, let's go!) nor drives the horse ("Walk on! Forward!) Rather, she simply walks on her way, relaxed and sure of her destination, and Kim accompanies her.

Understanding a Horse

The horizon calls

Perhaps you have experienced along with them the happiness and relief horses feel when their constantly restricted living space is enlarged a bit—their effusive, even explosive joy when they can leave the barn to run around in the riding arena, when they can go from the stall out into the open, when their room to move is enlarged in a new pasture. It is as though they are able to breathe deeply once more. Their bodies, as though suddenly awakened and filled with an inner music, revel in the greater freedom. As far as the eye can see, horses are starving for a wide open expanse. They cannot get enough of it. All horses, even old, lame and sick ones, hear the call of the steppe—the sight of such an area reawakens long-forgotten (or buried) feelings of power and pride, the fire of youth. The sight of open space, room to move, summons up euphoria, something a horse does not experience in his confined, cramped daily existence.

Everyday pressures

No matter how the daily life of a horse today looks, the direct interaction with human beings always means a massive additional shrinking of his space for movement and play. Even if a horse has to live his whole life in a closed space, in his box, he can at least turn and move around and hold his body as he pleases. But in work, we give him directions, exact to the centimeter, for every step, for positioning all his extremities, even the tip of his nose. Even when a person is riding a horse through the open countryside and allowing him an unforced posture, the horse is still not permitted to graze even though such tasty morsels are growing over there in the field. When all around him open meadows are tempting him to go for a wonderful gallop, the human being forbids it and he must, instead, trot on unpleasant gravel roads. How is a horse to understand this?

Toppur's Answer

Change of attitude

The person as an impediment to the horse: let's look at the photos on the previous pages from this point of view. In both, I stop Toppur's forward motion and limit his movement, and both times the stallion does what I want him to do, but his attitude it is quite different. In the first photo, it is quite apparent that he loses his energy and feels himself restricted and blocked, even though my signal is soft and considerate. In the second, everything happens very fast—his mane is flying, the flow of his movement bubbles upward instead of dissipating as it did before. What caused this difference? The first time, I gave the signal to stop just for the camera—there is no other reason than that for my behavior. Toppur follows my body signals out of loyalty and because of his fundamental decency, but he immediately loses enthusiasm and interest. Horses dislike practice without a purpose, no matter whether it is in the riding arena or on the trail. They feel stifled, suppressed, disempowered, and boredom sets in right away. Such commands only serve to reaffirm to the horse his "slave" status, and drive away the joy of being together.

In the second situation, my action was not motivated by a superficial reason, but from what was going on—in fact, Toppur himself triggered it. In that moment he wanted to run off, to put that wide open space to good use. Because I have learned to listen to horse language I received his silent message and stood in his way just before he could carry out this appealing idea. The reason for my reaction was authentic and could be understood by him—once again a human being does not have what it takes to keep up with horseplay. I

Between hard work sessions, rolling and wallowing are very relaxing. You should give it a try—it really does a body good!

calmed Toppur and finally tried to come up with alternatives. Although he puts off his own desires and instead follows me, he seems to keep his good mood. You can see by his playful expression that in this instance he was not miffed at having to stop.

At first glance these seem to be two very similar situations: a person conveys to a horse that he should stop, and he does. But, if we adopt the horse's point of view, there is a huge difference. In the first case, my action is arbitrary and has no genuine motive— from Toppur's perspective. In the second case, it has to do directly with me, with both of us. Even in relations between human beings, attempts at manipulation—putting the relationship to a test—can spoil a friendship, whereas a sincere opinion or request in no way clouds it.

Motivated and unmotivated actions

The Reality of the Other

There are many different ways to get a horse to comply with our wishes. What distinguishes them is the attitude and feelings of the participants. How is my horse dealing with this? Why am I doing what I am doing? Does this action have anything to do with my horse? Is there a purpose to it that he can understand? Meaningless actions on the part of the person are a sure way to quickly lose a horse's motivation. Who among us enjoys being ordered around? That is why it is so important to find clarity about that which remains unsaid and to search for the subtext of an action. Is our horse really a full partner in the discussion? Does he have the freedom to refuse my offer, and what do I do in that case? Does the horse's resistance or wanting his own way have negative consequences for him? What is really behind that "free, willing" obedience? Is the horse actually responding to pressure? "No, please—I don't want to be whipped, I'm galloping already!" "No, stop—no jabbing spurs. I'm already yielding!" "No, please, no pain in the mouth. I will halt immediately!" Or, is the horse responding to an invitation, a suggestion, a request? "Yes, good idea! We'll do that, let's go!" "Okay, I'll try it once, but you'll help me, right?" Look deeply: a gentle vocabulary and a quiet—to our ears— way of speaking may awaken trust in us, but the horses may understand that very differently. What did a horse learn when he learned to obey? Did he learn cooperation, or did he learn to submit to force and avoid pain?

What does the horse hear?

There is a rule in riding that the bit is only as harsh as the hardness of the hand on the rein, and I would like to add, as hard as the heart of the person to whom this hand belongs. Horses fear the latent aggression of a person at least as much as the actual physical pain. And they forgive children and unskilled adults the occasional clumsiness, as long as the person's intentions toward them are basically good. Horses sense intention. Freedom, and even its opposite, coercion, is not always obvious. In either/or thinking it could be dangerous to even imagine the horse having an active role. Being together is only possible with the horse's obedience. He who is not on the top is on the bottom. And because one's partner is a large strong horse one must fight for the dominant position with many tricks. Once a person has installed a power relationship between himself and his horse, he must never lose it. He must always have the upper hand. But that also means that his horse can never win.

There is always room for fun—like hopping around together. Feeling good, playing, being silly in the riding arena makes it a special place.

"Horses need strong leaders!" Even the vocabulary that is used to legitimize the absolute subjugation of the horse makes those whose hearing is more attuned cringe. There are still some people who remember and tell amusing stories about horses that—unlike our very uncooperative cars—Sunday after Sunday reliably and safely brought the carriage home with a their dead-drunk driver. Or, there is the one about the farmer who sat in the back of the cart getting a head start on cleaning the turnips while his horse pulled the cart through the village to market. The horse is not just a means of locomotion that we invented, but a living, thinking being in his own right. The very fact of his "aliveness" makes

A "strong leader"?

Freedom from the Very Beginning—The Foal

This Connemara foal came into the open arena, all on his own. Here he is making his first acquaintance with the noteworthy oddities of life with human beings: ropes, leading, allowing one's legs to be handled and picked up. He experiences these things step-by-step, cautious, in full consciousness. Giving his front feet to the person, an alien being, requires much trust, because the natural instinct of an animal of movement tells the foal that he must especially guard his legs. But then he even willingly allows this two-legged creature to take a grip on the hind leg. The soft press of the whip handle supports the young horse by keeping his attention on the rear part of his body and to consciously process the unaccustomed action. The foal is not pushed around but rather is already learning to understand human beings and to think along with them. To leave the horse a choice, to give him space in which to make a decision can never begin early enough. After all, interaction with a human being should not stand for force or even misunderstanding. Instead, it should mean new experiences, getting to know the world, and, perhaps making a special friend.

Freedom from the Very Beginning—The Child

Little Steffi and the great Kveikur: it cannot be exactly determined who has tamed whom here. The young gelding is a "wild one" but, to him his Steffi is just the coolest person in the world because she lets him be who he is, she understands him. Their affection is mutual. The two are one heart and one spirit.

total control impossible. It also means that he is independent and able to act for himself. He does not need anyone to push the buttons or turn the key. Perhaps we should put our trust in that—in the horses' and our aliveness, in their and our essential natures, in their intuition, and our own.

The Secret of Motivation

The space of freedom is the horse's space

The fundamental condition for a horse's well-being is freedom of movement, that is, to have at all times the opportunity to move in any direction. When I personally became conscious of the importance of free space in relationship to horses—and it was Reno who made this clear to me in his inimitable fashion—my work with them changed completely. Until then I had made an effort to constantly improve and to try to learn everywhere. Reno, however, negated each of my efforts with a sad sigh—an "unmotivated, lazy horse." With hindsight, I am so happy that he was so determined and that he consistently refused to accept something that was wrong. Otherwise I never would have found the right way, but he brought me to it. Because I could not manage to improve this horse's urge to go forward, I could not get rid of the feeling that something was wrong between us. These days, Reno motivates me. He pesters and cajoles until I relent and we head for the formerly oh-so-odious arena. Now it is his space—his practice space.

Free space —how it begins

Free space can mean many things to my horse: giant pastures, the arena, letting the horse lead, loose reins, tacking up at liberty, a person who backs away—but also one who doesn't! Whether or not something actually is free space as just defined depends on the special relationship between this person and this horse. What is always decisive is how free the horse feels. It is easiest to recognize this at the beginning when the lessons are first being put into practice. Did everything once begin with fear? Fear impresses itself upon them. Horses have decades-long memories for things that frightened them and can be depended upon to remember unpleasantness. Once the fear has been internalized, a minimal reminder will suffice because horses have a strongly developed avoidance reaction. They shy in the places where they were frightened—this tendency to do this is well known. That is why you should take great care at the start of the horse-human relationship. How should everything begin?

Do you find out how the horse feels about each new task—forced or encouraged; supported or driven? Another reason why beginning in free space is so crucial is because a horse's "yes" can never come from a relationship based on the principle of pain avoidance. Once beaten into him, the tendency to flee, or avoid pain, remains, and that means "no" in the language of horses.

Respect and Space

Who has space, and how much?

To be able to move at any time is a basic necessity of life for a horse. Horses need space in which to move freely in order to express themselves and also to feel safe. The physical aspect of space is the unrestricted freedom to move, and we human beings, too, know enough to treasure wide open space for that reason. It allows us to go here and there, wherever we wish, but also to move away from unpleasant things and leave them behind us. Another significant factor about free space, in a social connection, is that politeness and respect are expressed by consciously maintaining an appropriate distance. Space means power. The amount of space a person is allotted shows how much significance he has in his surroundings. Whether it is the larger office, the larger house, the greater distance maintained out of respect—he who is powerful demands and receives as much space as he wants. Giving someone space is one important way of showing that we acknowledge and respect him.

Developing self-trust and understanding

When it has become a matter of course for you to respect a horse as a unique individual, regardless of his age, looks, or abilities, you will be a welcome guest in the world of horses. But, for many people, the politeness they show to an individual is entirely dependent on status, and the one who seems subordinate is treated accordingly. To most people, an animal always counts for less than any human being. In particular, very young horses, whose undeveloped strength is still easily overcome by force, are handled with very little consideration. Free space, on the other hand, gives the young horse the opportunity to develop a far-reaching understanding and to become a confident and safe animal in his life with human beings. A child once burned avoids the fire—and an equine "child" is no different in that respect. He will remember forceful handling and painful experiences for the rest of his life. Once "broken," he will be forever shy of human beings. Instead of hurting or pressuring him with forceful measures we can win his trust and teach him how to think along with us.

Free space for children

At the same time, free space, with its opportunities for play, allows our own children a natural entrance into the world of horses. If children are taught to be in a command-giving relationship they can easily develop tyrannical behavior. The power over a large horse is only superficially beneficial. Children hardly ever adhere to rules—rather, they tend to be inconsistent. When there is free space such inconsistency is not harmful, because horses are also that way, and they like that quality. It suits them. The little girl in the photos on page 48 does what occurs to her in the moment she communicates with her young Icelandic gelding. She does it for him. He does not always understand everything that she says, and she does not always understand him. But, by her behavior and with her thoughts she asks him his opinion, and she is always clear in her affection. He is, too.

"A human being never feels more physically free, exalted, or favored than when on horseback, where he, an understanding, tactful rider, subjugates the powerful limbs of this magnificent creature to his own will, exactly as if they were his own, and so is able to travel as a higher being."
~Goethe

It is actually relatively easier for weaker people, or those who are inexperienced with horses, to take the first decisive step in communication—namely, truly and deliberately respecting the horse. Perhaps it is the natural shyness that this large, powerful being evokes in people who have not come to know him. So, they approach him carefully, with reserve and politely. It pays to find exactly this attentive "beginner's attitude" in yourself, because it is only when horses feel themselves respected that they become openly communicative. On the same level as the horse, equal to equal—this means doing nothing that the horse is not also permitted to do. A person who truly wants to live without force or violence must first deliberately practice complete non-violence himself. That is more easily said than done for someone who perhaps has trained himself for years in the language of power as a means of dealing with horses.

Trust and the Rider's Tact

The person who mounts a horse assumes a classic and oft cited position of power. He is the one who determines where the horse goes; he "takes the reins." He must learn to control his horse—and quickly, too, or it will become uncomfortable up there. The act of riding is a very intimate contact between person and horse that generally comes to be under unfortunate circumstances. The horse gets a strange burden on his back and cannot reject it, or disobey. His opinion does not count. He simply must do what he is told. The person leaves the security of the ground and is suddenly atop a much stronger living being whose thoughts and feelings are alien to him and upon whom he has no influence. This kind of beginning makes it highly unlikely that a close, empathetic connection—and a two-way connection at that—can exist. The stress on both parties is at a much too high level for

Beginning in Freedom

Riding in friendship: A beginner is totally overwhelmed by the prospect of forcing a resisting horse into submission. He has only his "feel" and considers himself fortunate when the horse helps him and meets him halfway. He needs a horse that seeks contact with him, who wants, of his own free will, to understand him. To begin with, he feels very insecure and unsure because he has entrusted the entire weight of his body to the mare who must move for both of them. But, the horse gladly carries this man. After all, she invited him onto her back! She resumes the dialog that the two of them had previously established on the ground.

that. The arrangement of "man on horse" allows no space, no respectful distance, no slow approach. So, a trusting familiarity, which can only be developed step-by-step in freedom, is not present. Emotional closeness is replaced by control. Though the rider may, after a while, master techniques that enable him to control his horse, that much-touted "feel" for horses, that is, the ability to put oneself in the horse's place is seldom activated.

The greatest joy on earth?

Good riding is sensitive. The good rider listens "into," and entrusts himself to his horse. This critical step comes more easily to the beginner than to the person for whom riding has become routine, because the beginner already feels overwhelmed by the task of controlling the large strong animal. To him it is all too clear that riding can become problematical when the horse is not in agreement with the venture. How it can look when the person's close contact is approved, even sought after by the horse, is shown in the series of photos on page 51. It can be clearly seen how rider and horse try to come into agreement with one another. In the first photo, one is asking the other. Then, when he is up on her back, Hazel asks her rider, and they are both in a lovely moment of equally sending and receiving. The activity changes, there is a dialog back and forth, they are both very concerned about one another: this is communicative riding from the very beginning.

Riding as dialog

Horsemanship—Free Space and Good "Feel"

A "feel" for horses will never be learned by someone who pressures, dominates, and controls. We learn this feel from the horses themselves, by observing, listening, and sensing. Horses are grateful for such passive, receptive awareness, and are enthusiastic teachers. They love to share themselves, and their readiness to make an effort, to wait patiently, and to forgive clumsiness or lack of skill is quite moving. The tale of the horse that exploits a person's every weakness originates in the everyday world of force-based relationships. Is it at all surprising that an animal uses any available possibility to escape from that? Given space, there is no need to resort to that kind of behavior at all.

Growing along with horses

Having more freedom of expression is certainly of benefit to the horse, but it also works to the advantage of the person involved. He, too, gains some freedom—to experiment, to play, to learn. Nothing has to succeed quickly, nothing is forced, everything happens in dialog with our partner. That means, too, that we can allow ourselves some mistakes because the horse has the freedom to offset or counterbalance them. The horse lets us know when something is not good for him, when we have missed the mark, or something is just not quite right. A communicative horse is an irreplaceable corrective. Anyone can make a mistake, no matter how experienced he is working with horses.

Play space is learning space

I now have an expert to help me discover what my horse wants and what contributes to his well-being—in fact, the best expert, is my horse himself. In the proper environment, all I need do is ask him what he feels like doing and what will do him good. No one can answer these questions for me better than he can. But, once again, I must always give my horse the space to withdraw if he chooses, and the freedom to express himself without interruption or contradiction. I must make a genuine choice possible. That is free space.

My horse knows best!

Balance in Communication

In a couple of pages you will see a photo sequence that is a direct continuation of the one in which I stopped the Icelandic stallion, Toppur, from running into the valley (see p. 41). Although I greatly restricted his movement, Toppur still retained his good mood. My action was motivated by genuine emotion, my "no" was authentic and not directed at him—and horses have a very fine sense of this frequency as they do with everything having to do with feeling. Despite the understandable reasons for my action it seemed to me to be a little bit like robbing Toppur of his freedom, so I tried to offer him the movement he had wanted. I run ahead up the hill. While doing so I mentally "lose sight" of Toppur and mislead myself into the false notion that horses always want to run. But now Toppur does not want to run fast, particularly because I had just told him that I did not feel up to running. At first he increases his concentration on his own body, listening into himself with turned back ears as he directs his attention to the movement itself. Lost in my misconception of what freedom means to a horse (as though freedom for a horse always means freedom to run), I do not perceive Toppur's real interest at that time and I wind up running away from him. In the third picture I apparently notice that something is not right. Of course! My horse needs help, feels "handicapped" with respect to running, is struggling with the different terrain, and needs encouragement...or so I think. So I again run away. At this point, Toppur could have become seriously offended—if someone is handicapped here, it certainly is not he. Instead, he turns the whole situation around, captures its comic aspect, and gets his revenge for the previous jerking around by my hands. It is a big surprise to me as he suddenly appears and overtakes me on my left.

Toppur's initiative brought the relationship between us back into equilibrium. After I ignored him several times, albeit with the best intentions, he participated more proactively in the conversation, instead of resignedly withdrawing. The horse's right to express himself freely creates the foundation of our relationship and is a fundamental requirement of our continuing journey together. Without this balance of communication between person and animal, everything else is impossible because it needs to build on the consciousness of freedom. Freedom is the basis of everything that follows in the coming chapters—free play, and our work freely done together.

Inner Space—Freedom within Ourselves

Our inner dimension as new space

Our inner attitude is a decisive factor in our relationship with horses. Do we give them inner space instead of assaulting them with demands? Do we make room in our hearts for them? Or do we use them to satisfy our hunger for freedom as we unconcernedly live out our dreams on their back? He who wants to create space for horses despite his own constant human presence needs to first have freedom within himself. Freedom for horses begins in us. Instead of blocking their way, making them yield, driving and stopping them, instead of wanting to constantly and in every conceivable way manipulate them, we must open a "feeling" place within ourselves for them. The airier and more boundless this inner space is the more joyful and winged the horses become in our presence.

Horse senses something new

The miracle begins when we no longer demand anything from our horses but instead try to create as much freedom for them as we possibly can, particularly in our presence. At first, the horse is relieved that no demands are forthcoming. Then, perhaps, he is a bit puzzled: "What is this? Here is someone who wants to do something with me yet asks nothing! How strange!" His interest is awakened. "You, a human being, are giving me space, are making room for me?!" He senses that he will discover something new here, as when a door suddenly opens onto a vast, spacious expanse which beckons him to step into it.

A joyous space

Only when I am able to "release" my horse, not just physically but also in spirit, can he feel free in my presence. I must free my horse within myself. Only when I give him this inner space will he speak to me there. The greatest freedom we can give our horses in these times is invisible to outside observers. But our horses sense it clearly and respond accordingly.

Tunnel Vision

Going downhill, the pace becomes too fast for me so I decide to run back uphill with Toppur. In these photos you see what happens next after the "abrupt halt" scene on page 41. I turn uphill and run ahead. In my thoughts I am already ahead of myself, or more accurately, behind the present moment. My thought is that Toppur would like a quick pace, so that is what I offer him. I run ahead of him so he has no choice but to come after me "because out in public Imke always wants us horses on a line. And now she's thinking that my lagging behind has something to do with that ditch..." In the third photo, I am looking behind me because Toppur is not keeping up the way I had expected. Actually, this has nothing to do with the terrain, but rather with me and my misconception. Instead of getting angry, Toppur sees the amusing side of following me. He positions himself behind me and assumes what is clearly a driving posture as if he were a stallion directing his herd. You can see it in the fifth photo. I notice absolutely nothing of this. Human beings have tunnel vision! Toppur finds that particularly funny and amuses himself at my expense: the stallion suddenly and surprisingly switches sides and, bucking enthusiastically, takes the lead. "Now will she finally notice?"

"To be truly alive means being involved in life's constant encounters."

~Martin Buber

ON THE SAME WAVELENGTH— Playing Together

The Grey Horse's Dance

A sharp crack tears through the air. Someone person has entered the large arena, which moments before belonged to the horse alone. The person makes noise, cracks the whip. The grey horse's heart beats faster..."Hey, you!" No doubt now, the person means him. It is his turn now!

Not so long ago this was like a nightmare for this grey Iberian. As soon as he came into a riding arena, anxiety gripped him and he lost control of his body. He could no longer stand still, he began to sweat from sheer upset, and wound himself up more and more—all before anyone even thought of riding him. It only became worse the more he was made to move. The more that human beings demanded control, the more he fell apart. He was an impressive animal and looked brilliant during movement, and many admired his proud beauty. But, even the gentlest dressage was now a horror for him and this anxiety would start with grooming and tacking-up. He was not lacking in talent—on the contrary, he had exceptional physical ability, and had been to excellent trainers. But the grey hated what people did with him, he hated the fear and the stress, and there was no way out of this pressure.

This horse once hated everything that we did with him. Here he flies easily over the obstacle, his expression relaxed, happy. He enjoys playing together and follows his person everywhere, backward and forward, and at every speed and rhythm. His previous mistrust has been transformed into unreserved enthusiasm—healing through play.

Now, his heart beats fast because a person is coming toward him and calling "Hey, come on!" The grey horse stands there at liberty, motionless, and proud until he suddenly takes off, straight across the huge arena. Like a stroke of white lightening he streaks across the black sand to this person who calls him. "Here I am," he seems to say. Eyes flashing, the horse stops in front of me and waits for me to continue the game. I run off, the grey enthusiastically running behind me: around and over jumps, kicking up his heels—the horse is always faster. Once again he catches up and then passes me. I laugh enthusiastically, he snakes his head happily. Now he circles around me—larger circles, smaller ones—he seems to be wrapping me up. "Great, super!" He chews a bit of carrot, then leaps along behind me again, and rises powerfully into a levade with good flexion. He offers these movements out of pure pleasure. Now his legs buckle, he goes to the ground and enjoys a good roll back and forth in the dirt. He looks bold. Meandering, jumping, rushing off in a gallop and coming back in an impressive trot—to this horse our time together is glorious, wonderful, abandoned play. Nevertheless, behind it all is a serious thing for both of us—we are playing with his fears. The crack of the whip, collection, being ridden—all these were once very frightening things for him. People had put extreme pressure on this very sensitive creature, cultivated his battle of desperation in high level dressage lessons.

It is over! Gone! All of that is no more! Never again! The grey horse snakes his head vigorously, his leaps into the air are like a dance. It is in play that this horse reassures himself over and over again that he is free. Play is medicine for his spirit.

The Balance of the Relationship

Creating a playroom

What does it mean to play with horses? And how do we arrive at such interaction? In the last chapter we discussed the importance of giving the horse space—as much as possible. So that a dialog of movement could come to be, we initiated the giving. We made room for the horse and brought in various freedoms. In doing that we helped to balance out a bit the real lack of freedom in a horse's life. When the "superior" two-legged partner makes

himself less obtrusive and gives the horse some of his own free space, he makes it possible for man and horse to be on a more similar level. If the horse accepts this offer of space it can quickly expand to be large enough to accommodate play—the initiative lies with the horse. At the end of the last chapter the Icelandic stallion Toppur became proactive because I had unconsciously severed the connection between us and was running away from him. He reestablished our connection by switching roles and amusing himself over my solitary "lead horse" position. It is here, in the balance of the relationship between man and horse, that we find the beginnings of play. The equality of the partners is the basic requirement for fairness—the same opportunities and rights for all players. Our playing can be truly carefree only when things are fair.

Here a young horse is playing all by himself, full of energy and the joy of life, taking pleasure in his own body, and in harmony with himself.

Horses often play with one another. When they do, happy expressions and "game faces" like these are typical, particularly the two horses in the background.

What Is Your Game?

Types of play

"Playing," what a friendly word! Every one of us associates it with good feelings. It promises fun, being carefree, enjoyment, good spirits, cheerfulness, and companionship. Games are a source and symbol of friendship. We become happy in play, and playful when happy. There are countless ways to play, and play itself is creative. As we play, new ways to enjoy ourselves arise. We can play by ourselves, all alone, turned outward in high spirits or absorbedly inward, lost in the depths of a quiet game. But, the majority of our games involve more than one player—"team" games. So when we think of playing, when we use the term "game," we usually think of happy togetherness, a game in the company of friends, of playmates, of game partners. And there is also the one-sided "game" that is played at the expense of others, a nasty game that only one side finds amusing—and the other, though it may put a good face on things, wishes himself far, far away.

Unlimited Games

"Feeling good" games

Even animals passionately love to play. Games are an important part of their lives, at least when they feel well and happy. Not only youngsters but adults, too, play with one another. Animals also play by themselves or against "opponents." What interests us here is companionable play that is fun for all the participants. We know that people can play with other people on this basis, and horses with other horses but can a person and a horse play with each other? Naturally, these could not be ridden games, like a gymkhana, but rather

A game between a man and a horse—fun and joy for both of them! The happy expression of the Haflinger speaks volumes—even obvious to the person who is not yet familiar with various horse expressions.

must be animal-oriented games, ones that have a similar appeal to both the person and the horse. Both participants have fun, just as when we run around with a dog, or when a cat plays with us. And the invitation to play often does not originate with the person but with the animal. However, we live more closely with our dogs and cats; they stay with us because they want to. It is different with horses. They are not with us of their own free will. Without fences, they would be gone. Is it even possible for horses and people to play with each other in such a mutually enjoyable way?

Games have their own language, order, and beauty. Games have such a great power to attract that they can be fascinating to experience even when you are just an observer.

Playing with horses

When horses play with each other in the field, they attract attention. Passers-by stop in their tracks. What would it be like if could take part in these games ourselves? What if our horses invited us to be a participant and play along? Such a game, such play, would be an act of social togetherness that transcends the boundaries between species. It is this special type of play with which we will concern ourselves in this book.

On the Spirit of the Game

What is a game? When is an action "playing"? How is play different from other activities?

Is there a game in the air?

In order to more closely define the nature of play, it almost seems easier to begin with its opposite. What is very definitely not a game? What stops us from playing? We are hardly in the mood for carefree play when, for example, we are ill. The joy of play requires that we have some excess energy. If we are feeling weak or ill, we need all of our strength just to get through our everyday activity. We have little left over for playing, because playing is a "luxury." Playing is an activity without a direct practical purpose. It is done simply "because"—out of mood and desire. So, part of playing is a certain feeling of well-being coupled with a measure of excess energy.

In addition, in order for a game to take place the atmosphere must be right. This is a very important element. Where fear or enmity is the predominant emotion, there is no

Here you see the beginning of a game between Toppur and me. It is reminiscent of the circling game the young stallions are playing in the photo on page 8, where each tries to pinch the other on his hind legs. As a human being though, I am relying on the horse to restrain himself and not use all his strength. Therefore, I initiate the action carefully and at a distance, because I require a "polite" game. At the same time though, I have an advantage in this situation in that I have Toppur hanging on the end of a rope. He does not have his full freedom of movement, so I must give him extra space and make room for him. I must cordially invite him and clearly yield to him. Otherwise Toppur could easily feel pressured, interpreting my offer as force, and then the playful atmosphere would be snuffed out.

room for play. We need a certain sense of safety and feel carefree in order to play. Games exist and survive only in a friendly, agreeable "climate."

So, playing requires energy, a safe and friendly atmosphere, and harmony. These elements of every game must be there as a foundation before we even begin. At the same time, these elements will be developed and increased through our playing together, and our relationships overall will be strengthened.

Depending on desire and mood?

Energy, friendship, overriding harmony—what do these mean in practice with horses? How do we recognize these elements? How do they manifest themselves?

Once you have experienced the feeling of genuine connection, you will never again want to do without it. Trophies, ribbons, the cheers of the crowd—how shallow all these are in the face of this deep joy of playing with your horse. Friendship does not ripen in chains, between "you must" and "you'll be sorry if you don't." Friendship means that we understand one another, that we belong together. From the joy in each other's presence a game develops. "How lovely that you are here! Don't run away! Stay here with me!" Here is El Paso with his Astrid.

A Threesome Playing

It is the end of October, but the day is warm and summer-like. Max and Atila already have their winter coats. They feel lethargic and do not have the desire to do much of anything. It was so warm in the indoor arena that we all immediately broke out in a sweat. Then Max had the idea of the three of us going to the driving arena—it is gigantic, and at the edges there is even a bit of grass. It is right next to the indoor school, so off we went. We began a game with each other, or rather many games, always new ones. First Max, the small bay, challenges me, then the grey Lusitano. The two horses take turns, one of them always offers to play while the other grazes or waits a moment until the urge to play grabs him again and he decides to participate too. So the players change up—sometimes one horse plays with me, sometimes the other. But in between the two geldings play with each other (you saw them on page 11) so that I, too, can have my rest periods.

Riding, rolling, rearing games, galloping together neck-and-neck—we play in every variation. We all play as long as we want, each of us has fun in his own way.

Regulated Play

Battle or play?

When horses attack one another even inexperienced people can discern relatively quickly whether it is meant in fun or bitter earnest. Certainly the wild games of over-enthusiastic horses are impressive in their display of sheer power. But a genuine fight between two horses is something very different. Just the sound of an enraged horse has a primal force. The experience of seeing and hearing a fighting horse leaves us no doubt that what is going on is not a game.

In addition, the expressions of the animals tell us a great deal about their mood and attitude. We can read their emotions even if they are not making much noise at the moment—at least, just as with people when we know the individuals involved. With good friends we know immediately whether something is intended seriously or not—with strangers it might take us longer. Horses, too, are individuals in the way they express themselves. But they signal their joy in playing with a particular, more or less distinct, facial expression: their "play face," which you can see many times in the photos in this book. The horse stretches his upper lip forward, and has a happy, eager look, similar to his "grooming face" when an itch is being scratched exactly right, or when he gives himself a body rub up against a tree trunk, for example. The difference is that when playing, the horse's attention is more outwardly directed rather than focused on his inner well-being. This distinctive and pronounced expression of pleasure does not constantly or necessarily accompany all playful activities—even people do not laugh all the time or turn the corners

The "play face"—an expression of enthusiasm

of their mouths upward in a smile while playing. But, once you have begun to pay attention to the silent expressions of horses you will frequently notice this look of enjoyment, this "play face." Even the thought of playing can be sufficient to evoke this expression, as shown here in the photos of our white Iberian Atila as he gets in the mood for play.

Even if you are not familiar with horses' expressions, by watching them even for a little while you will be able to tell the difference between playing and fighting. A game—whether between horses or people—has a certain order to it. There are set regulations: the rules of the game. This "regularity," this adherence to rules, can be seen in horses, too, even if we are not particularly knowledgeable or experienced horsemen.

That playful feeling: When you observe horses more closely, you begin to be able to see what they are thinking. At this moment a generally reserved horse is getting the urge to play. In the first photo on page 64 he is still undecided. Should he wait until someone challenges him? "Oh, but the two of them over there are playing so nicely..." Then the mood seizes him: "Now I'm going to play too—otherwise they'll have all the fun without me!" His eyes flash, his upper lip is saucily stretched forward, and he trots off to the other side of the riding arena: "I want to play, too, please!"

Back-and-forth play

A game adheres to a certain order. Horse games are generally "tit for tat" or like for like. Among horses, the response to an action is another action just like it: rearing is met with rearing, neck biting with neck biting, bucking with bucking. The partners always act reciprocally and adapt themselves to the other's level of energy. With the small, shy youngster the games are gentle, with the self-confident rowdy, the games are rough. The balance between the partners is always maintained.

In principle one can play alone, but as soon as more players take part in a game definite rules become necessary so that the prerequisites mentioned at the beginning will continue to apply to everyone involved and no one feels pressured or over-challenged. The fundamental elements of play—energy, safety, a friendly atmosphere—are maintained for all participants by this regulated equilibrium even if there is playful conflict. Social distinctions and varying methods and abilities to exercise power are blunted by the rules of fair play.

Male animals in particular, regardless of species, value the protected play situation because in this framework they can very safely test their strength and compare it to others'. A horse can practice, learn, and act "as if" without negative consequences, even if he is occasionally "defeated." The rules of fair play must be adhered to by all participants. Whoever plays unfairly will soon be unable to find any partners. As soon as someone plays as though the rules do not apply to him, the game has basically died; one player becomes the "plaything" of the other who "plays games" with him, who exploits him or "plays him out." Desire, joy, and a feeling of well-being are then one-sided. The game has deteriorated into a power play.

The framework for play

A mutual game, therefore, can only exist because of the conduct of the players, and it is always only an offer that can be accepted or refused. Participation is free-willed, and voluntary—an agreement to play cannot be coerced or exist one-sidedly. All the players have given their agreement and all their opinions count equally.

Foul Play

Fair play or power play?

When a person truly wants to play with a horse and relate to him as a partner, he must adhere to the rules. Otherwise the horse remains a plaything, a toy that the person merely uses to play out his own game. If I "frighten" my horse away in play, then he can frighten me away—equal opportunities for all. It is particularly important to maintain this equality. Interaction between man and horse is generally defined by such a rigid hierarchy, that it is difficult to find a rider who will meet his equine counterpart on an equal level. But only when this happens will a horse understand that this is supposed to be a real game, that is, one that he too can enjoy.

The more independent and self-confident a horse, the more readily he will withdraw from a game when he doesn't understand its purpose, a "game" that is just for the human gain. In the worst case he will even become aggressive as the result of such "pseudo" games, because he has had enough, and in addition to feeling oppressed he also feels himself tricked, like the victim of a hoax. When there is a power play, when authority is being exercised, the horse becomes a plaything. Do we really expect him to willingly grin and bear it? If a person retains his "master" position when he decides to play, then the horse must play along regardless of whether he wants to or not. As said, the rules of the game are the basis of fair play. When a person does not acknowledge and adhere to these rules, then his "game" becomes "foul play." We like to give nice sounding names to not-so-nice realities. The "fun" in such foul play is our fun only, and will stay that way. When the horse's opinion does not count, when there is no room for his freedom and his wishes, when his fears and anxieties are not heard and acknowledged, no genuine game can exist.

The Rules of the Game

Mutual play takes place within a protected framework made possible by (among other things) the validity of special rules. All participants adhere to these rules, which are in effect during the whole game.

When several different partners want to play with one another:

- *All should have the same rights. For the duration of the game all participants have the same status.*
- *All concerned should be agreeable to playing. No one can be forced into it. A genuine game is an offer, an invitation. Everyone participates voluntarily.*
- *The manner of play is adapted to the weakest player. If the game becomes too rough for him, he stops.*
- *Anyone can leave the game at any time.*

Horseplay

The most important element of playing together is equality.

Of course it is quite possible that even the horse's natural social behavior in this area has been perverted. If so, then he cannot really play, or he continually switches back and forth between playing and being in earnest. Kim was such a horse. When he came to us he seemed to be obsessed with play. He was under extreme pressure, but at the same time so inhibited that he could barely move. He did not know what to do with the pressure. Playing, as he understood it, was a way of venting—but at the expense of the other

A game can look like this, too. These two discovered riding together and have incorporated it into their mutual play. Icelandic gelding Kveikur loves it when he has his Steffi all to himself and can carry her off. For her part, Steffi uses the time on Kveikur's back to recover from their crazy games—Kveikur is always faster. So, through riding, everything is evened out again.

horses who became victims of his obsession. Kim did not dare to approach higher ranking horses, but he "played" with all the others whether they wanted to participate or not. It was evident that he "over-played" rather than truly experiencing carefree joy. At the time Kim was an insecure and clumsy horse with a negative image of himself. Because of his behavior he was not very well liked in our herd. He forced his games on the others with no consideration at all for them. If one of them could not or would not play along, Kim became furious and kept pressuring him. In the end the "playmate" was further beaten up when Kim became annoyed at the refusal to "play" along any more. Really, you could not call this play. Kim did not adhere to game rules, broke through resistance, did not accept refusals and acted out with force.

"A human being plays only when he is most human in the full meaning of the word, and he is only fully human when he plays."
~Friedrich Schiller

Play should be free from hierarchy. The same rights apply to each participant. The little foal goes ahead and cheekily bites the strong stallion in the neck. The stallion playfully snaps back at him and the two of them begin nipping at one another. Older, higher ranking horses can be attacked without fear during play. There is no respectful distance to be maintained. Differences in rank no longer count. In the protected play environment a weak horse can "assault" a strong one without fear of punishment because the stronger horse will not use his full power, but rather respond in a similar, playful way. The stronger horse will never become enraged at the "disrespectful" behavior of his attacker. A correction or reprimand would be a sudden breaking of the framework of the game and a shock for the weaker horse whose security depends solely on the rules of the play situation. Playing makes all the participants equal for the duration of play, and the rules of the game provide a framework, much like a contract, whereby the game can come into existence. Play occurs on a common level, where all are equal. This applies also to games between a person and a horse. Remember how, at the beginning of this chapter, Toppur playfully got revenge so that we were even again?

At the Edge of the Arena—Toppur and Shannon

As these two stallions thundered by, our alert photographer, Bernd, captured them with his camera. So, we can leisurely study exactly what is happening here.

Shannon, the young bay, gallops shoulder-to-shoulder with Toppur. He playfully bites Toppur in the neck, and after this attack, tries to overtake Toppur in the next stride. Toppur throws up his head and neck, musters some momentum, and gets his revenge, just as the youngster, believing himself to be the victor, thinks, "Now I've got you!" Are we witnessing a battle for rank and a correction of the lower ranking horse? Not at all! Certainly the two stallions are racing and the younger (by four years) Shannon "attacks" Toppur, the boss, in order to throw him off his stride. But look at the faces of the two of them, especially at the point where they are interfering with one another. It is a wild game. Like two adolescents who romp together, shove one another and laugh about it, these two are enjoying their racing and fighting. They are buddies!

If you study the photos closely you will notice something else, namely that the two stallions are running in exactly the same rhythm and tempo, even though they are in a full gallop. Their friendly relationship is reflected in the exact unison of their movement. Something becomes visible here that will be very important for us later on—shared rhythm.

In the Riding Arena—Kim and Hans-Peter

Horses will also try to synchronize movement when they are playing with human beings. Here is a photo sequence of Kim, a Haflinger, that shows how he adapts himself to his human playmate, even though he is so full of power and enthusiasm that he is nearly bursting out of his skin. Nevertheless he listens to his friend. Hans-Peter takes one energetic jump and then, in the next step, he tones down his movement and with a slight gesture of his fingers, asks the horse closely following to bear with him. It is not easy for Kim to adapt to the constant stopping and starting, particularly because he must also control his own high level of energy. He does though, tossing his head playfully. The rhythm remains completely harmonious, even though the play is quite heated. Kim is teeming with strength and playfulness and is right next to Hans-Peter. Again, compare the leg positions of these two playmates.

In the Riding Arena—Kim and Waltraud

On this day Kim chose yet another human playmate: Waltraud. She is very pleased that Kim has challenged her to play. It is her first time doing something like this, so she is excited at the invitation to play such an extraordinary game. She hops through the sand and repeatedly leaps into the air. Kim accompanies her, but at first he is a bit disconcerted by Waltraud's leaps and is not quite certain how to respond to this movement. "I have never experienced anything like this wild rhythm. What am I supposed to do with it?" Kim seems to ask as he observes Waltraud for quite some time. Then he finds the solution for himself. He responds to the hops and leaps of this twirling woman with flying canter changes that are just as energetic and expressive. Back and forth they go. In the photo on this page, Kim has just switched back to the left lead.

When Two Do the Same Thing—Playful Harmony

The central theme of mutual play is the equality of all participants. At first this equality is just an understanding but in the course of the game this conceptual framework also becomes outwardly visible. It is reflected by all the participants—in their body carriage, in the rhythm of movement, in their identical reciprocal actions, and in a mutually agreed upon level of excitement, even including muscle tension, a total physical harmony. Play partners match one another. They find a common rhythm. They follow, respond to, and accompany one another. Instinctively, involuntarily, their rhythm, tempo, pace and momentum are synchronized and their movements are adapted to one another. Such simultaneous, identical action does not exist only at play. We also see it in other social situations. People who understand each other very well will often, as though coincidentally, do exactly the same thing, reach for an object at the same moment, begin talking at the same time, or even try to telephone one another at the same instant. The synchronization of rhythm is not simply there from the onset—except between mother and child in that first special time right after birth, or maybe, with love at first sight. Otherwise synchronization must develop and can be lost again. For it to exist there must be empathy and receptiveness to the moods and rhythms of the other. Only an intimate emotional connection makes such simultaneous action possible.

Social unity

Rhythm, Tempo, Momentum—and Empathy

Harmony of movement

Can such harmony be intentionally created? The rhythm of body language is a language in its own right, and is determined by emotions and the unconscious. Something similar happens in our spoken language. Here too, the rhythm is influenced this way. Without noticing it, or meaning to do it, people talking to one another match each other in tone and rapidity of speech. If we are not successful in this (even if only a little bit) uneasiness remains that "something" was not quite right with the conversation—with oneself, the other, or maybe the subject. Somehow the warmth between us was lacking.

The rhythm of the unconscious

The matching-up—or lack of it—in spoken language is something we can perhaps perceive if we consciously look for it. Perhaps we can also intentionally, carefully match up to the other person. This can be a dangerous maneuver because the deliberate attempt to assume a partner's tone, pitch, speech rhythm or dialect can completely misfire should the other person notice and suspect that it is deliberate. Then the chance of harmony may be lost forever. One-sided manipulation of far-reaching unconscious processes is seen as an attempt to deceive. So much for spoken language: what is a just delicate issue becomes totally impossible in the language of body rhythm. It is too quick for the eye, the differences are too subtle. The attempt to consciously match up to another, to synchronize the waves of individual rhythm, tempo and momentum cannot succeed. It leads to being "blocked" and has the same effect as when, in the middle of a rhythmic dance, one partner suddenly tries to stiffly break down the individual steps. We cannot perceive these common rhythms through conscious observation. Only photos or video clips can reveal them to us—an exciting possibility!

Let us dance and play!

Riding the Same Wave

Playing together lets this kind of harmony come to be, just like dancing. Yes, the attraction of any game lies in the unconscious synchronization of rhythm, whether by clapping, hopping, chanting or foot stomping. All participants move in rhythm and as though carried

Here is a "gentleman" from the four-legged oversight committee. There are always witnesses. All the work in this project is open. The communicative horses closely observe what transpires in the arena and check to see that all participants adhere to the rules of play. Interestingly, the horses seem to have agreed among themselves never to soil the arena. None of them ever leaves any manure behind to be cleaned up. And this habit seems to be passed on to others, because even guest horses and newcomers follow it after a short time. The horse that enters this space does so with dignity. The human being who does so, and observes the horses' rules, makes himself a welcome guest of the horses.

Harmony makes many things easier

along on the same wave. The individual energies of the participants no longer work in isolation or against one another but rather, they work together. Instead of restricting each other, the overall energy accumulates and grows stronger. The whole becomes greater than the sum of its parts. Each individual participant experiences an increase in power.

Because playing together enables the participants to "attune" to one another, it unifies and strengthens. Our sense of belonging and well-being in the company of others is determined by the harmonious interplay of speech and movement rhythms. However, these shared rhythms cannot be produced one-sidedly or deliberately. Just as they work on our unconscious, they also are directed by our unconscious. Harmonious, perfectly synchronized movement requires emotions that are in harmony and perfectly in synch. Empathy and overriding unity cannot be forced.

Horses are very receptive to our rhythms because they use this form of communication much more intensively than we do. Horses get information about the minds of others, even members of other species, this way. Soundlessly, matter-of-factly they communicate with others like this. But above all, horses simply like to move in synch with one another in intimate interaction. They appreciate the increased energy that arises from the overriding unity. Horses act together. Often and with pleasure they move in synch, trot in the same rhythm, canter alongside one another in the same footfall. Horses even try to adapt themselves to human beings if they find us sympathetic. In this way, we can bring them with us into new movements, previously unknown to them.

Passaro and His Sitting Game

This is the story of a game—a game that makes it easier for us, human and horse, to be together. It was discovered as a way to come to grips with threatening moods so that we could then work together again in a relaxed manner. This is the Sitting Game, discovered by Passaro, the horse sitting in the photo at right. I hesitate here as I try to describe him. He is a horse somewhere between genius and sheer madness, fragile and delicate as a mimosa, yet violent. Any effort at influence or manipulation upsets him greatly, enrages him and makes him aggressive. He is one of those very few horses who intentionally seek revenge for what was done to him. They were bitter experiences that taught him his art of fighting.

Passaro is a highly traumatized horse. He was last in a leasing barn in France where Kirsten bought him as he was bound for slaughter. Many people had tried to break this horse's resistance. Despite beatings, hunger, and riding him until he collapsed, Passaro's spirit did not bend. On the contrary, he learned to see through the deceit, dirty tricks, and "false fronts" of humans; he learned that these creatures are weak and afraid if he only can just wait for the right moment.

It is not exactly child's play to get such an abused horse to participate willingly in activities with human beings. But Passaro's compromised health made it necessary for us to work with him, and he wanted to participate once he realized that it helped him. But how could he do this, and what could we do, when every sort of human influence was so abhorrent to him? He became enraged about whatever we tried to do with him and he became enraged when we did nothing. "Please wash me, but woe to you if you get me wet!!" It was a dilemma intensified by the fact that our work does not proceed from the prior subjugation of the horse, but rather, from winning his friendship and empowering him right from the start. Passaro's abilities to fight grew immeasurably. Sometimes things became so impossible that Kirsten no longer felt safe in the arena with him. But, her departure only made him even angrier. It could not go on like this. So one day, when Kirsten had fled in fear, Passaro simply sat down after a brief roll and did not stand up again until Kirsten, full of concern that something must be wrong with him, came back into the arena. Just like that, he realized he had a way to bring her back.

Do not think for a minute that someone had taught Passaro to sit like this in the circus style. We would not have survived the attempt. Even to think of it would have been a punishable offence in his eyes, and to actually approach him with ropes and reins...well, it would be easier to take on a world champion karate expert. Nor had Passaro observed another horse sitting down—this was his own discovery. And it works beautifully! Kirsten immediately hurries back and asks him if he would like to stand up again because it breaks her heart to see him that way—the unusual posture cannot be good for him. The effect on Kirsten is increased if one delicately splays a hind leg. Passaro makes himself immobile, small, un-dangerous, and almost a little bit comical only to bring Kirsten back into the arena with him.

In the beginning, Passaro sat down only when his overflowing power and excitement had driven Kirsten away. Then, apparently, he discovered that sitting calmed him. So now, when it seems necessary to him, he intentionally employs this movement for the pleasant effect it has on his own psyche. He uses his Sitting Game to rein himself in, to cool off his overheated temperament and to maintain self-control. We cannot forget that Passaro has understood all his life how to use his knowledge and abilities to his advantage—more on that later.

The fact is that these days Passaro will sit down as soon as he notices that he is in "too deep" and the powerful physical and emotional sensations engendered by his work might become too much for him. The tension, which grows with increasing collection and finds its explosive expression in that crown jewel of haute école, the capriole, is now no longer threatening to Passaro. This is how he gets himself under control. He uses his Sitting

The Sitting Game controls excitement that is in danger of bubbling over. "Very calmly now, first sit down, breathe deeply and everything will be fine." What a moving sight this horse is as he sits there, peaceful and harmless.

Game and then we can continue working. "Keep cool, old boy. Sit down for a bit." We get the impression that he is more concerned with our well-being than his own when he does this. After all, his rages were more likely to be a danger to the people around him than to himself. At any rate, Passaro began this game for Kirsten, so that she would feel safe staying with him, and these days he uses his game to hold his inner demons in check.

Certainly Passaro is not a normal horse. Those who know him know that he is as outrageous as his ideas. But Passaro solved our mutual problem in a very creative, successful manner, and now nothing stands in the way of his further development.

Perhaps some time when you find yourself in a social situation that threatens to spin out of control because every person involved feels himself attacked by the others, because everyone's nerves are frayed like those of a newly captured band of horses, you will, in the midst of the tumult, think of Passaro's idea and his Sitting Game will come to mind. "Before we go on, let us sit for a while. Let us sit and calm down. Then we can see how to proceed." I do not think Passaro would object if some human beings adopted his strategy.

The Power of Play

A place between the worlds

In play we find ourselves, for a certain time, in another world, beyond our everyday cares and conflicts; in a space where normal power relationships no longer apply, and even battles are fun, simply because we are playing. We are only pretending when we fight. What happens here does not become disastrous as in "real life." Having "play space" requires that the game does not become too serious for any of us, and even horses are careful to honor this framework. Playing should not have any negative consequences. That way, we can experiment, take risks, try new things. In play we can enjoy the connection with each other and gain access to new opportunities for experimenting with different behaviors. Play offers the chance for creativity, inspiration, and healing. Boundaries that kept us trapped, dissolve. Playing lets us grow closer to one another because it overcomes differences—even when they are as great as between man and horse. If there is a common language, we can find ways to play that are fun for all participants, even when we belong to different species. Through play we come to understand each other more and more. We become like-minded—we become playmates. Play removes the distance between us and lets us become one. We get a glimpse into the other's world of thoughts, even if the other is an animal, because play conquers even the boundaries between species.

And suddenly everything is okay!

Again and again, things are returned to balance during play—a common equilibrium is continually sought. So ensues an instinctive feeling of belonging together. We feel kinship with the other. He is the same, he follows the same rules. Play strengthens the connection between us. During play we were on the same wavelength, we showed each other fairness, and in doing so, we proved that we follow rules and are therefore reliable partners. Play creates congeniality. We play with those whom we like, and we like those with whom we play. The play atmosphere is conducive to friendship. We have had fun together. This experience remains long after the framework of the game has fallen away and we have returned to our daily routine.

The beginning of friendship

Playing together creates team spirit and bonding—a sense of belonging together. As we continue on our way we will not forget the energy, the lightness, and the carefree feeling of the game. No matter where we are, we can always find our way back to the joy, harmony and liberation that are there for us without limit. After all, we can at any time, let the game come alive again among us. We will remain bonded to one another, even if we now turn our effort to a particular end—and work with our combined powers toward a new goal.

The Transition

Toppur is getting into high gear. Playing is great fun for him and incites him to more. In the first photo his movement is a bit confrontational and directed right toward me. So, I very clearly and deliberately back off and guide the stallion so that we come to be alongside one another. The playfully intended head-to-head confrontation has become side-by-side accompaniment. Neither confrontation nor competition is the goal of our togetherness—but rather, friendship, accompaniment, companionship. Toppur does not yet know this—at least not for certain. He senses that I want something from him, that I am looking for a stronger connection to him, but what for? "Why is she looking at me like that, is she challenging me? Apparently not, but then...what?"

"Perhaps we dominate other living beings so well only because we are unable to communicate."

~Elisabeth Marshall Thomas

A NEW GOAL: Working Together

From the Horse's Point of View

The nature and history of the horse

There are three obstacles that make it difficult for us to work with horses and we will thoroughly deal with them in this next section.

The first difficulty lies in the horse's nature. Work, or comparable behavior, is not foreseen in its life plan. So we have to create something brand new if we want to work together.

Secondly, for thousands of years the relationship between man and horse has been burdened by the fact that the sole purpose of the relationship was to harness the horse's energy for human endeavor. The power required for work was taken from the horse. Understandably, a horse will try whenever possible to avoid a situation in which he is constantly deprived of his energy.

Our understanding of work

A third obstacle is our current understanding of work: it requires great effort, it is sweat-producing, and it must be very serious. So, it is the pure opposite of joy, play and exuberance. This general way of thinking is very obstructive because horses see things completely differently.

What makes work so problematical?

We cannot reasonably expect that our horse will allow himself to be moved by us to do something that, from his point of view, entails only disadvantages for him. To get to the point where a horse wants to work with us, the negative aspects of work must be transformed to positive ones. Only when the horse can sense that it is advantageous for him to work will he stop trying to avoid it. On the contrary, he will happily anticipate work sessions.

This is the point on our path where we depart completely from the normal, typical relationship between man and horse. From the horse's point of view, the sort of work that is geared solely for the interests of the human, that takes possession of the horse's body, that oppresses and exploits him, should never have a right to exist.

The Art of Working Together

About competition-free play

Here is where the spirits separate. From the horse's point of view, there can be no work together unless it is useful to him and strengthens him. Cooperation with humans must have the best interests of the horse as its focal point. This is the only kind of work that interests us here, and the only kind of work that has a place in this book.

Working without an agenda or in pursuit of a goal, and in the interests of the horse is an idea that is not in its essence all that new. Wherever riding became an art—not just a way of moving forward over the ground but having value in and of itself—man found his way to the horse. The horse became the measure of the craft instead of just the means to an end. His well-being was suddenly the heart of the matter, or put another way, the work served only the horse.

Further on in our journey through this book knowledgeable riders will encounter some things—exercises, arena figures, aids—that may seem familiar. It is very important that we do not depart from the "path of the horse" with these things that we learned when we had another point of view. Whether shoulder-in, travers, or piaffe—only when we retain the horse's point of view, and we stay on his side, can the differences between an aid and force, challenge and over-facing, gymnastic and torture, joyful working together

Just a moment ago we were still playing. Suddenly we discovered an exercise—travers—and worked together toward our common goal, in a very focused way. Here the mare, Hazel, is learning a totally new (for her) way of placing her feet. She works on the exercise; I am there to help.

and zombie-like resignation be recognized. The well-being of the horse as a measure of the horseman's art: we have had such riding in our culture from time to time. Even the quotation at the beginning of this book from one of the last great masters of riding art, is an expression of such a sensibility.

On the Way to Work

Work as personal training

In the beginning, the transition from play to work is not easy for a horse to understand. In nature a horse does not have to do much more for his sustenance than lower his head—his behavior has no influence on the amount of food available to him. With the exception of pawing in deep snow to get to some grass the horse's "work" is not the finding of sustenance but rather, unlocking the nutrition. Because of his extremely long, voluminous and complicated digestive system, the horse utilizes a variety of low-energy plants and extracts what is necessary himself, just as other animals obtain their food through industrious collection or skilled hunting. A human being, too, requires prolonged, goal-oriented activity to get his sustenance. To a horse, on the other hand, such a concept of work is completely alien. The idea of "earning his keep" originates in our world and is incomprehensible to him.

An entryway for human and horse

So, it is all the more important that my horse trusts me when we begin work because our relationship now enters a critical phase. But, we are not totally unprepared. The unity of play has created a certain security and we have been careful to concentrate on playing games in which we are in alignment, where we match movements. In these, the idea of competition recedes into the background. This can be seen in the photo sequence with Toppur in the transition to this chapter on page 79 as we switched to moving side by side. Such games can create security for this new phase in which we confront our playmate in all seriousness, critique his actions, and encroach on his personal space. The unity achieved during play improves our transition into this unfamiliar concept of work, because when someone feels acknowledged and recognized as an equal he is much more open to constructive critique. We want to pull in the same direction during our work, not act in opposition to one another.

"In his physical exertions a human being has the freedom to rest as soon as his efforts become painful to him. For a horse that is not the case. We have ways to force him to keep working, so that after a time it becomes necessary for him to take for himself, through apparent rebellion, the rest that should have been given him simply by the decency of the rider. It is easy to understand that this is not the way to strengthen the muscles and tendons. It exhausts him and is the primary cause of his eventual ruin."

~Ludwig Hünersdorf, Hessian Riding Master, 1791

A Conversation with Toppur—Part 1

The whip moves toward the stallion's hindquarters. "What is that about? What do you want? Oh no...you want to do something...again? I know all about that. You people are always like that. Leave me alone. I want to get away from here. The path leads straight ahead."

"Wait, Toppur! Wait just a sec."

"I don't want to anymore. Let me go to my friends."

"Wait, Toppur, please—just wait one moment. I did not mean it that way. I did not mean to give you an order or pull you around. I did not want to spoil your fun... really not."

"So why did you do it?"

"I'm sorry. Please excuse me. I had an idea...I noticed something back there. I would very much like to show you. May I?"

Toward the Horse's Goal

Strictly speaking, any kind of work is unnatural for horses. But, if we do not merely burden the horse with our kind of work but rather offer him something oriented toward horses' goals, his eagerness to work will be difficult to restrain. Of course, these goals must be comprehensible and worthy of the horse's striving if they are going to determine the course of the work, and a horse show win is not particularly desirable from a horse's point of view. If a horse understands the purpose of our work he can experience it as a very personal kind of help and learn to appreciate it. Suddenly he discovers something brand new in being with his person that he finds increasingly interesting—this is about his own well-being! From the playful encounters at the beginning a focused way of working soon develops.

This goal-oriented mutual activity takes place only with the support of a human being. While horses can play just with one another, they need our presence and inspiration for this process. We two, person and horse, work together on one thing, we strive toward a goal—the horse's goal—that is a fascinating and completely new experience for our horse. After all, he can play horse games without the company of a human being, but here all sorts of unexpected possibilities are being offered. Working with a person provides an opportunity to learn in an entirely new way. Horses can become positively addicted to this kind of work and they begin to demand it more emphatically than they do their daily feed ration.

How this work looks, how it differs from conventional training and why the horses become so keen for it is what the next chapters are about. But we, like our horse, do not yet know what our chances are for such work. We barely have an idea of how something like this will proceed, so in the beginning, it is not easy for us to find a way to transition into it. Actually, we would prefer to remain in the previous chapter and play together there.

Now, you who are reading this book only need to leaf through some more pages and see that this totally new form of work can become more concrete. But your horse can easily become irritated at this stage, especially if he is mistrustful because of his prior experiences. He does not know yet what is in store for him. So, like our Icelandic stallion, Toppur, he will ask, "Why is she doing this? What in the world does she want from me?!"

What Is Wrong with Work?

Working free willingly?

Any rider with even a little experience knows that a horse does not work for people of his own free will, but rather requires a certain force to make him comply, even if, in public, we would prefer to say just the opposite. The more honest such a person is the stranger it must seem to him that there are supposedly horses who, independently and voluntarily, work on even the most difficult exercises like piaffe and passage.

Why do these horses so willingly do such strenuous things? And (this question is perhaps the most painful) why are the horses that we know not also like this?

A few steps back in time

To better understand the current state of affairs between horses and humans, to illuminate what is possible, and impossible, about it, we will now examine how things came to be this way and what went on before. To do this, we will take a few steps back into our shared history and look more closely at it as it concerns work.

It was not so long ago that the daily life of people was unimaginable without the labor of horses. Their service was needed wherever strength and speed greater than a human being's were required. With the help of horses continents were conquered, wars were waged, innumerable burdens carried. The horse served as weapon, transportation, carrier

Working as a Threesome

Is it play, or is it work? These horses let one flow into the other. They make no distinction and switch seamlessly between phases that are quite in earnest and those that are playful. Sometimes all three of us enthusiastically tear off together and simply fool around. Sometimes there are individual issues that become a theme for the work and move into the forefront of our activities—problems that we then work on in the midst of our play. For example, both of these horses have a troubled relationship with the whip, and both are afraid of being ridden. These subjects are problematic for them. The complete freedom and the quality of the energy of our playful atmosphere give them so much security and strength that they can address the wounds of the past.

"I will not be hounded with the whip here," Max reassures himself, and then accepts the touch of the whip as an offered aid. Confident and self-possessed, he assumes an upright posture as his Lusitano friend looks on. And the grey horse does not move his hindquarters away from the whip or flee, but rather, moves toward the person working with him. A short time later he carefully begins to move into collection and in doing so works on a deep trauma—his fear of being trapped: unfortunately, riders today think of collection as driving a horse they have deliberately incited into close confinement of some sort, whether of tightly held reins, or against the arena wall. This puts intense pressure on a horse and not only has adverse physical consequences, but does profound psychological damage as well.

"No one is forcing me, I am doing this for myself." Atila tries the first careful steps of piaffe. Meanwhile, Max grazes in the background. Again and again the two horses switch from concentrated work to more playful activity, and then return with the lightness of play to the previously stressful situation that they can now serenely master.

A working animal

of cargo—a multi-purpose, grass-run engine that worked day after day without complaint. Naturally the horses were often inexorably exploited until they completely broke down. At the same time, the human beings with them worked nearly as hard. But, unlike people, the horses labored and suffered for reasons that they did not in the least understand—to say nothing of consent. After all, human beings needed them.

As machinery began to replace horse power, it seemed to those who had a heart for the horse, that this was deliverance for these animals. At last the forced hard labor was over. Finally, no one would out of necessity treat them badly. Interaction with horses could become a luxury, riding a way for horse lovers to pass the time.

Yet horses have received very little in the way of deliverance. This change of circumstances never penetrated far enough into human consciousness to change the basic relationship between man and horse. It is almost shocking how much the horse is still seen by people as a creature intended for their use—completely different from a dog or cat. A horse is not seen as friend or companion. At best, that is just an "add-on" to the utility aspect. In human consciousness the horse is here to be used and as a matter of course, to be totally at the service of the whims of mankind. As a bicycle is for cycling, a horse is here to be ridden! As I was bringing a yearling to the pasture a three-year-old girl asked me, in wonderment, why no one was sitting on the horse, and if he was still too small for that, well, a child could be put on his back. Even picture books teach our offspring that on a horse's back, there belongs a rider. A human being lays claim to this body so invitingly made for use. He marvels at the aesthetics of the horse and literally wants to straddle such beauty and power. The body of a horse belongs solely to his legitimate owner, which the human being considers himself to be. He has acquired the horse and with that he has brought the right to demand whatever sort of work he wants from "its" body. It would be preferable if the horse, of "its" own free will, gave up every right to any sort of power, individuality, independence, and self-determination, but if it has to be, the human will by force maintain mastery over his possession. "What's the matter? Is that not a riding horse? Can we not

But, that is a riding horse!

How would it be?

Imagine you have no car to bring home the bags of groceries from the supermarket, nor any other form of transportation. You have no little house in the country, no condo in the city, not even a rental apartment somewhere. You have no permanent roof over your head at all. Night after night you must find a place to sleep outside. You have no house, no bed, no stocked refrigerator, no winter clothes, and not even a single piece of paper.

You have nothing except what you brought into this world—your body, your skin. What a life!

You are happy. The sky is endless and the earth lies at your feet. Wherever you want to go your legs carry you. Your dense coat protects you from the weather. The wind streams through your hair and whispers ancient tales. All of nature is always there for you. Food grows everywhere, you only need to take it... Everything is given to you.

This is how horses live.

THE LEVADE—
THE ELEVATED HORSE
When work makes a horse feel great, he will feel that work is great. That is the secret of motivation!

sit on it? Then why aren't you riding?" Riding seems to be an inherent right of human beings—and this animal has been brought into the world to be ridden. Even "nature freaks" and animal protectionists foster no doubts about it. The right to ride is not up for debate.

Good Old Tradition

We human beings of today are no longer dependent on the services of the horse. That also means that we no longer need to concern ourselves with his care; the individual horse and his health are no longer necessary to our lives. A rider used to need his horse: "it" was a tool that had to remain functional. The mounted herdsman needed his horse to keep the cattle together and perhaps also to "cut" individual animals or to catch them. Perhaps he even needed the help of his horse to keep a raging bull in check. The more exacting and dangerous the task, the more indispensable was the individual horse: a horse that had learned to accept and fulfill such tasks was very valuable to his rider. In the best instances, man and horse worked together because the horse understood the whole job, thought about the work and willingly participated in completing the task. He performed this service in the person's interest, but for both of them—even for the rider—it was work. Rider and horse lived as well as worked together. The daily toil was necessary for survival. They shared the hard life with one another.

Teamwork in working life

Today such situations are rare. A horse no longer works with a human being: "it" works for him, while the person amuses himself. Horse and person no longer share very much, whether bread or work—and certainly not pleasure.

"It is impossible to control a horse that has not previously acknowledged its rider as Master, that is to say if it is not fearful, and because of its fear, obedient. A horse gives you its obedience only out of love of itself, in order to avoid the punishment that would otherwise be unfailingly forthcoming, even if it only unintentionally failed to obey. It cannot be trained with kindness because it would still hold too much to its own will, but if it is fearful it will stay by me and I can direct it as I please because I am its Master."

~William Cavendish, Duke of Newcastle, 1667

The world of horses and its peaceful rhythms are very alien to today's man. He lives fast, shrill and loud, and everything must function at the push of a button. He climbs out of his car and onto his horse and off they go. He wants to have his fun during his scarce leisure time, he wants to pursue his pleasure, and his horse serves that purpose. That is why horses and human beings are further apart today than ever. What to the rider is sport, fun, and restorative is to the horse, hard work, senseless running around and all too often, torturous stress. The health of horses suffers from this—totally unnecessarily, and it is a situation that, strictly speaking, violates our animal welfare laws.

The horse as partner

The work horse has become a sport and leisure-time apparatus. Horses as consumer products? It almost seems that way. Today horses are used up much faster than in the past, and are considered old when they have fundamentally just reached maturity. In the past one simply could not afford to use up a horse in its youth. Horses were intended to perform important and valuable work for many long years. To this day—despite all noble sentiment—the egocentric viewpoint of human beings toward the so usable horse has not changed one whit.

> *"If the horse does not obey then someone should hit it as hard as possible with a whip or a stick. In this way it will not only jump as high as it was first asked to but much higher than is necessary at the moment. Subsequently you will no longer have to beat it—rather it will jump as soon as it sees someone approaching behind it...and this, in short, will hold true for all of riding."*
>
> *~Xenophon 400 BC*

In Search of Motivation

In recent years more and more riders and horse lovers have considered how riding could be done in a way that is more considerate of horses, how they could motivate their horses to want to work, and what horse-oriented training should look like. So, very quickly, a number of training methods incorporating some of these aspects appeared on the market.

But the problem with work cannot be solved with methods, be they ever so natural, artful, or artificial. Seen from the horses' point of view the problem lies much deeper: no matter what kind of work the human being does with them, it remains something that is forced on them, whether harshly or more gently. No matter what the particulars of the work, one thing always remains the same—horses are not asked for their consent.

The problem lies deeper

If we examine the current training of horses by people we find a classic example of negative motivation. The horse does something because he wants to avoid a negative consequence that the human being will inflict on him. The horse avoids something of which he is afraid or has learned to fear, and this "something" hangs in connection with an action of the human being. He runs so that he will not be attacked, so that the whip will not strike him, so that the spurs won't prick him. He stops so that his jaw will not be crushed, so that he will not be hit on the nose, or so that he will not again be chased round and round until he is totally exhausted. Horses try to avoid things that are unpleasant. Flinging out his forelegs so that no one whacks his sacrum, jumping high so that the pole does not hit those sensitive legs, running because someone is sitting on his neck, faster, faster...Horses love to work, or do they?

The strategy of evasion

And If You Are Not Willing...

Throughout history "carrot and stick" have governed a horse's training. These paired concepts were so commonly used that they have found their way into our everyday speech in areas that have nothing whatever to do with horses. "Carrot" and "stick" have become

Punishment and "reward"

synonymous with "reward" and "punishment," with attraction and intimidation, with positive or negative motivation. The question here is: how do I get someone to do something for me that he does not want to do of his own volition? We are talking about manipulation—of either the gentle or harsh variety.

Traditionally, the stick reigns in the relationship between man and horse because a horse acts to avoid unpleasant consequences, not in order to get something for which it is worth striving. He reacts to the negative reinforcement, he is worked until he gives in, yields, or moves forward. The horse learns about negative motivation and wants to avoid something worse. The reward is that the unpleasantness stops as the person lessens his actions. The carrot is not typically used in horse training. Only in trick training and a few other training methods is the horse systematically given an additional food reward.

Generally, dressage training with food is not considered serious training. If you only offer your horse an inducement or lure him with food you are ultimately dependent on his good will or his hunger. So (the thinking goes) it is better to show dominance to which the horse must yield many, many times, until he does without resistance what is demanded.

A sweet treat...What's this—a mistake being rewarded?! There is no "wrong" between us. What counts is making the effort to understand.

Shane and the Tire

Shane is two years old. He, too, urgently wants his turn in the arena, our work area, but he wonders, "What can I do here, so young and inexperienced?" I have an idea and get a tire and put it in the sand. "Look, a tire." Shane looks at the thing and peeks inside. I ask him if maybe he would like to put a foot in it. "My foot?" Shane is confused—what an idea! His mother had always warned him to be careful of his feet so that they would not come to harm by his stepping in a hole. He makes a half try but does not trust himself. That thing is just too bizarre. On the other hand, he is now a bit sad and stands in front of the tire not knowing what to do next.

"Should we try it one more time? Look Shane, the edge is not sharp, it gives—it is not dangerous." Shane thoroughly inspects the tire once more, and tries again to fulfill my request. He gets as close as possible, his hooves next to the edge, then he shifts his balance backward so that his head is directly over the hole. As I ask him again I realize that I am now asking too much. He would gladly do what I want but he simply cannot. "You were super! Wait, I have something for you! Now look, we'll do something completely different—we'll roll the tire between your legs. Wow! Terrific! How brave of you!"

"Thank you, Shane. You are a terrific horse!"

Questioning the Purpose

At the end of this chapter, as we shall see, Toppur does walk on the curved line. After a hesitation phase he decides to go along with my suggestion on a trial basis, so to speak. But at first, he does not take up my suggestion: Toppur retreats in response to my actions and refuses to comply with my request.

If we regard a horse as a free being, it is very important to respect him unreservedly in such a situation, along with his refusal. Here comes an alien creature and demands something. "Why should I do that? I see no sense in it."

"Because you must!"

"Because you must!" The person who gives his horse this answer may win his horse's obedience, at least insofar as the horse understands and is able to carry out the instruction. However, the horse's enthusiasm and independence will be lost forever.

"Would you perhaps try it just once?"

The more independent our horse is the more quickly he will question the purpose of the work. Our answer to his question is crucial, because with it we set the course of our relationship. "Because I say so." This answer, emphatically given to the horse, reveals the two-legged dictator. So, all that went before is really just a prelude to this. Even the answer, "Because there is a barrel standing there," or, "Because there is a tire on the ground," does not change the dictatorial drift. It merely defers the more concrete answer, "And I want you to go around this barrel." Despite everything, horses can—perhaps after a period of hesitation—decide to go along with their person's new idea, even if there are many reasons not to. It is one of the wonders I wish to tell you about in this book. Despite everything, horses will go along with us, all on their own, of their own free will, just because we do not obstinately try to force them. I do not have to assert my will, but nevertheless, my horse complies. That is a great gift. The answer that I give Toppur in this instance is, "Because I think it is important, and because I would very much like it." Instead of using pressure or exercising power I do exactly the opposite. I ask my horse to please simply try it.

"All learning is play."
~Plato

So Toppur ultimately goes along with my idea without knowing what it all means. He seems quite happy doing it even though he was so hesitant at the beginning. In the next chapter, we will look more closely at this decision-making process. Why does a horse do such an unexplained new thing at our bidding, this thing that makes not even a bit of sense to him—even though he does not have to and even though he does not want to? How does he get to the turning point? How do we lead him through the phase of hesitation? These questions are answered for us by Shane, a young Connemara stallion, who like his grown-up friend and mentor, Toppur, has a very independent, impeccably honest character. We see Shane in an everyday situation that is particularly problematical for him: he is confronted by a task that from his perspective simply cannot be done. You can read his story on page 95.

The Meaning of Little Things

Were you able to comprehend the dialog between Shane and me in the photo sequence on pages 94 and 95? It began when I wanted to show this young stallion that the tire is so totally harmless that one can even put a foot in it. That is how I imagined the session would go and that is how our work together could have looked. Shane, however, did not put his foot in the tire. But, he listened to me, tried to understand me, and did understand what I was asking. On a purely superficial physical level we did not succeed, but our work together brought us much closer on a mental and spiritual level.

Shane's feelings

In the first two photos, Shane, at my urging, is examining this movable "hole in the ground," which is quite sinister. Notice how he first leans away from the tire, his body evidencing mistrust and his clamped tail also expressing his insecurity. In the second photo, a short while later, he is relaxing and leaning toward the tire: his body weight rests on the right legs, he is more trusting, his tail hangs loosely, and even his hindquarters look different—the croup has changed position even though Shane has not moved one foot.

We can also see that Shane first stands at an angle to the tire, but then approaches it frontally. He would like to do what I want. Despite everything, though, the courage for the last step fails him. This horse that is so particularly sensitive to everything beneath his feet—he is somewhat "ground shy." Shane understands very well what it is I want, and

"Thank you, Shane!"

he gets as close to the rubber creation as he possibly can. He even crosses over it and comes back again, but he just cannot bring himself to step into the tire. That disappoints him, he shows some mild stress—it is a kind of inner withdrawal that, in typical pony fashion, makes him look rather sleepy. He shuts off. He is over-faced by the task of stepping into the tire. But, must he do this? Shane did all he could. He confronted a personal difficulty in a very focused way, just because I asked him to. He did not flee or refuse. He gave his best. He came as close as possible to the dark hole: it is easy to see in the photos how he concentrated on the tire problem. Shane went to his limits—at my request. What more could I want?

An Inner Language

As I was writing up the photo sequence of young Shane I noticed my hand gestures. At first glance they seem to direct the horse and make quite clear what I want him to do. Is the horse perhaps responding to this kind of hand gesture or sign language? A human observer, at any rate, could rely on my hand signals this way. But could Shane, a virtually green young horse that follows just a few minimal hand movements? It would be difficult even for some dogs to understand such a signal at the first attempt.

Mental pictures

My gesture accompanies what I am saying and a person may get quite a bit from that. But a horse is not as hand- or word-oriented as a human being. Shane is not paying attention to that. Had I used the very same gesture but thought something else—for example, had I concentrated on my own movements rather than on Shane and his feelings—the horse would have behaved completely differently. Apparently, Shane is responding here to what I am envisioning. How did I relay that to him? To communicate with one another we human beings use our speech, and for understanding we need to have words in common or commonly understood signs. Sometimes we also "speak" with our hands and feet, but that too is an external language. Shane pays as little attention to my hands as to my words, yet he knows exactly what it is I would like him to do.

The understanding between this young stallion and me does not derive from physical gestures or specific signals. Only one single time does Shane pay attention to what my hands are doing. You can see it in the photo on page 92. He knows this gesture of mine. It is a signal to him that I will, in all likelihood, very soon pull a treat out of my pocket for him. I am certain that he also knew this in other ways even before I made my intention so clear to him.

The principle of unity

To make it easier for you to participate in this conversation between Shane and myself, I put it into words. And it helps me, too, to talk to my horse in such a situation because that way I keep my thoughts on the matter at hand. But words and gestures are for communication between humans. The communication between a person and a horse occurs on a much deeper, more direct level. It eludes a formal observer. Such an encounter follows the principles of overriding unity that we learned to recognize in the harmonious dance of playing together. There the synchronized leg movements made clear that person and horse were walking together in harmony. Here the interplay between them is not so easily visible.

The melody is an inner one and that is where we both hear it. The way I move my hands is just a visible accompaniment to my mental images. With exactly the same body movement on my part, but different images for my inner eye that meant nothing to him, Shane probably would have walked away after a short while. The resonance would have been lacking. A horse perceives the whole of a human being and only when we are congruent as a whole will a horse understand and trust us. Therefore it is very important that we do not suddenly become conflicted or incongruent within ourselves when we want to work with a horse. If we do, we give up the spiritual connection between us because we strike a false note.

Although I have no physical hold on the horse, he picks up on the inner language of my thoughts and desires, and orients himself to them. When there is great emotional unity human beings, too, can pick up on each other's inner images. Suddenly we "just know" what the other is thinking in the very moment he thinks it, sometimes without even seeing him. We all once lived in a world without words, and as children, we could think and communicate using inner images. It was only much later that we began to orient ourselves to words. You too can understand this inner language if you build a feeling-based connection to horses—and you are already doing exactly that as you follow the horses here through the pages of this book.

Empathy

The Gift of a Labor of Love?

Shane tries to stay in step with my mental images: this situation is similar in its overriding unity and harmony to that of the running games Kim plays with his human partner. Shane's effort to make my expectations a reality does not quite succeed: the young stallion fears the dark hole, which is how he perceives the tire, and he cannot shake off his misgivings. You who have accompanied us this far will understand how important it is neither to pressure the horse nor leave him all alone at this point. A person who insists that the horse overcome his fears can quickly lose him, because when he lets his horse just stand there while he himself keeps his inner distance and sticks to his agenda, he demonstrates that success is more important to him than his horse. Such behavior is true poison to any relationship. A horse has tried his best to read our innermost desires and to act on them. A person who does not wholeheartedly appreciate such an effort has no business being around horses! In a situation like this, we must connect with our horse as quickly as possible so that he does not withdraw emotionally or become resigned. We do this by making our joy in his try very apparent, by clearly expressing our gratitude (giving some food is nothing other than this), and by immediately offering another alternative—an achievable task (like the "test of courage" with the rolling tire). It is extremely important to be clear about how sensitive such a situation is. This kind of behavior by the horse is a great gift to the person. How do you suppose the horse feels when his person does not even notice his gift, or complains about it, or wants to correct it just because the result did not perfectly suit him in that moment?

Staying engaged with the horse

Ultimately it is totally unimportant whether or not Shane actually puts one of his feet into the center of the tire. I started the exercise because I had noticed his "ground shyness." And it was precisely this insecurity that Shane confronted so intensively during our session. It is not as though Shane absolutely needs a tire encircling his feet for his continued survival. The tire is not the point of the exercise—it is intended to be merely an aid for Shane. The exercise was for his benefit. The focal point of our work, in fact, the sole reason for it, is the horse.

What do I actually want?

The Horse as the Heart of Our Work

In our work we try to be useful to the horse and to further his development. Does not dressage riding also have this ideal? Is it not said that dressage serves the well-being of the horse and is beneficial to his health? Horses should be advanced and further developed. Gymnastic exercises, collection, and "throughness" ostensibly serve that purpose. But, if we dig deeper, we soon realize that dressage is not about the horse himself, but rather

Hazel Learns Travers

The art of transformation lies in improving a horse's sense of his own body and in conveying a new experience of it to him. Sometimes this looks very similar to typical dressage exercises! Hazel, the bay Connemara mare, showed us travers earlier on page 80. How did that movement come about?

In travers, a horse moves forward and sideways in the direction he is bent toward. Hazel had never performed such a movement. In the first photo on this page, I invite Hazel to come toward me by offering her my space and inwardly freeing myself (can you see that I am making myself smaller?) Hazel is not quite certain whether she should accept the invitation—she thinks the whip and my raised arms might be arguing against it.

Notice how, as the process unfolds, understanding travels through the whole horse. At first her head has understood, but her shoulders (her forehand) are still saying "better stay away." At this stage her hindquarters are not very involved at all. In the second photo, the mare moves toward me with her forehand. She crosses the left foreleg over the right. Her indecision has been placed further back onto the hindquarters and we can clearly read the hesitation by looking at her left hind leg. But, once she has taken another sideways step in front she shifts her weight to her right and her left hind leg comes too! Her next step is actually one shown earlier on page 80. Note, the whole time my whip is directed toward Hazel's croup—not because I want her to yield there (as she still thought at the start of the exercise) but rather that she stays aware of her inner (here, the right) hindquarter. It is not, as is so commonly believed, the "leg crossing" that makes this exercise so useful but rather the way the inner hind leg takes on the body's weight and carries it in the new direction. The horse learns how to control his center of gravity and his balance while directing his body mass sideways. This is exactly how we developed this new movement together.

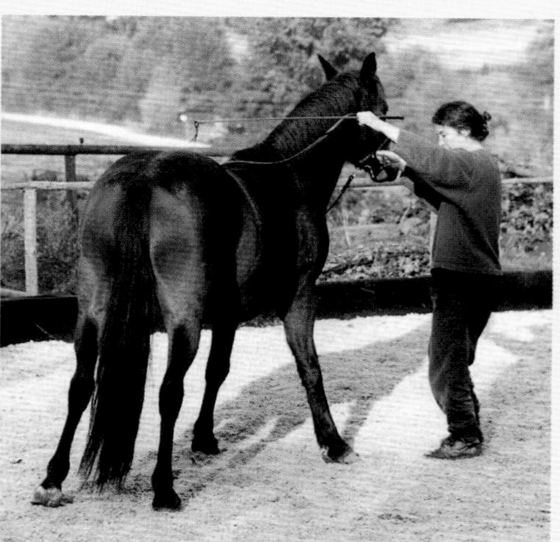

about the cultivation and conservation of his power to work. We find that, here too, the actual goal is to derive maximum use from the individual animal, only it is done with a strategically planned program. That is how it was conceptualized. But, many modern day dressage riders lack both the patience and the knowledge for such a program, and the reality of their practice looks very different than intended: the exercises are forced from the horse. Often, any method is deemed okay if it is successful—and today success is not measured in the horse's long-term soundness and ability to work. What counts these days is winning competitions, for which arbitrary, specific sequences of movements are practiced that are summoned from the horse with no sense of context or connection. It is not an unfolding empowering process that is wanted but rather, the mechanization of the horse. To a rider who takes seriously the ideals of dressage a good show result might be a "side effect" of his work, but it can never be the reason for doing what he does.

Dressage as drill

"Forward"—"Faster"—"Look right"—"Head high"—"Rear end inside...Oh yes, you will!"—"Halt! No, squarely, feet parallel!"—"Three steps backward! Don't drag your feet, make an effort!"—"Faster (different gait)"—"Wrong foot!"—"Halt!"—"Faster (same gait)!"—"Left!"—"Right!"—"Left!"—"Right!"—"Head inside!"—"Head down!"—"Slower (different gait)!"—"Stand still!"

If, as an experiment, we translate into words what a rider conveys to his horse while working him, it is easy to see that we are not on a dance floor here, but rather in an exercise class. The dashes between the words signify aids, corrections, punishments. Only a moment each for the rider, but for the horse it goes on endlessly.

The horse as modeling clay

Sadly, dressage today often does not mean working together with a horse. The rider works his horse, meaning he "works on" his horse. He focuses on his horse's mistakes and tries to remove these with strenuous grinding. He decides what is right and what is wrong. His perception of the mistakes comes from superficial, external criteria that are alien to horses. For example, the rider finds his riding animal stiffer when going to the right because the horse is reluctant to go in this direction. So, the rider practices more frequently in this direction and works on correcting his horse's disobedience by bending him more sharply to the right. Perhaps he also wants to have the horse's hindquarters more active in canter and perhaps he wants to build up the animal's back and neck muscles. He does exercises for these and maybe even uses special reins that are supposed to bring him nearer to his goal. The rider tries to shape the horse according to his will, however well (or badly) he understands "good form."

Riding art and horse work

Working together, working with a horse, is something different. I do not have an ideal form in mind into which I will try to mold my horse. After all, this is a living being standing here with me, not lifeless "material" that can and may be worked on as I please. The art of horsemanship as I understand it can only be an art dedicated to horses. This art must serve the horse instead of human ambition, performance, or the entertainment of the masses. What we want is for a good enough connection to exist between person and horse so that understanding and harmony rule. We want a hierarchy-free, joyful atmosphere—the same atmosphere that exists when we play together. Only under these conditions can I offer a horse something new: actions that are focused work for the horse and aids that are truly helpful. "Is there something you would like to improve? Are you perhaps not feeling quite okay there?" From play we draw forth the energy and the self-confidence to confront such sore points. A horse needs courage for this, even perhaps enthusiasm.

Artistic Temperament

The horse as the artist and the person as the assistant who helps him in his artistic endeavors, this is the relationship that Passaro clearly and gladly demonstrates for us. He has the say here! I am supposed to give the appropriate aids—in the correct way. If I have not given them in perfectly measured "doses" and have instead "pushed" (as shown here), the "Creative One's" concentration is disturbed. "Just a moment, please! This is not how it goes! I cannot work like this!"

I must beg for forgiveness. After appropriate homage has been paid, the Maestro arises, full of dignity.

Horseplay, horse work, horse art—after Passaro has collected himself he once again picks up the work and tinkers some more with his passage. I am allowed to assist.

Changing Roles

The horse works now, benefits later...

In "A Conversation with Toppur—Part 1" that started on page 83, Toppur shows us the exciting, critical moment when the person wants to switch from carefree play to goal-directed work. Working together is new to the horse—something he does not know in this form. No wonder he has reservations not comprehending the sense and purpose of such work together. The fact that Toppur nevertheless so readily and willingly cooperates, listens to me, and tries to translate my suggestions into action is to his credit, not mine.

The transition to work cannot be demanded. That, as the horse makes clear to us, will mean a parting of ways. It is at this point that we can lose the most valuable reason for undertaking this journey to begin with—namely, our horse. He withdraws—he wants to leave, to flee from us and this incomprehensible pressure. Of course, most of the time horses cannot actually flee from the situation and the person's pressure makes that even more emphatic. The horse's suppressed flight response is now held in his body, in contracted muscles, shortened, choppy movements, in a dreadfully high head, a tortured-looking mouth wide open...Oh no, this is not what we wanted.

And that is why we will not do this. We will stop when our horse says: "No!" We will let it all go, try another way, or do something else. We will not force our horse to do it our way. Rather, we will find the path our horse wants to travel and walk it with him. We ask him for his permission, we discuss things, and above all, we listen. "Okay, Toppur. Pardon me. I did not mean it like that." We reflect on the matter once more—pause—and then I make a renewed attempt. Now Toppur does what I request! He actually uses his hindquarters more because I suggested it. Was what I wanted clear to him from the start when I switched from our friendly game?

Still more questions

As soon as a horse has discovered how useful and helpful it can be to work with a human being, the transition to work will no longer be a problem. On the contrary! The horses profit from both work and play, will switch back and forth between one and the other on their own, and barely distinguish between one and the other anymore. The little bay horse, Max, and the grey, Atila seen on photo spreads on pages 62 and 63 are now in this state. And the longer the path is that we have traveled together, the more our work with one another has evolved and come to resemble our own art form, the more our roles will change. The work becomes the horse's thing, he creates the art. He develops clear ideas of what his person's presence means and what should come of it. He demands serious work from us: "Please, no silly games, let us get to the point." The person becomes a tutor who assists his horse—and a guiding principle of classical horsemanship, expressed in the words, "the horse seeks the aids," finally becomes a living reality. We will have more to say about that later.

Horseplay becomes horse work

The Second Part of the Conversation—Toppur Turns

In the beginning, the transition from play to work is not so easy for our horse to understand. So, Toppur was disappointed at my request because he does not want to be "worked on." We stop and I try to convey to him that it was only a suggestion, that I had a useful idea and good intentions. Thereafter we try once more, and I make an effort to show him what I mean. "How would it be if you used your haunches more when you move on a curved line?" Toppur makes a visible effort and does as I wish. Did the stallion really understand the purpose of my request? What is the point of doing this thing with the haunches?

Work must make sense to a horse. If I critique a horse's way of going, I want my comment to be accepted as I intended it. Who would allow himself to be judged if he felt himself at a disadvantage to begin with? Unfortunately, it is like this when we are outside because in this day and age man rules even in nature. My suggestion would have been understandable to the stallion if it were given somewhere else. We would have had more freedom and a more relaxed atmosphere in the riding arena. So, later, we will have this conversation with Toppur there. If you would like to join us, we will meet in the next chapter, in the riding arena, in the center of a circle.

"At the still point of the turning world...

There the dance is...

Except for the point, the still point,

There would be no dance, and there

is only the dance!"

~T. S. Eliot

On the Art of Moving in a Circle

The Horse—A Creature of Movement

Movement is the horse's element. Barely born, he is already on his legs practicing the primary art of horses—moving. His four feet are his priceless treasure. If he knows how to use them cleverly and safely he can, light-footedly, escape all dangers. Developing security in movement is his life's mission. "Learn to place your legs correctly" whispers his inner voice. "You can see your two forelegs, but you must learn to feel your hind feet." The inner voice is ever more urgent: "Learn to walk! Learn to run! Learn to feel!" The little horse grows, becomes bigger, heavier...He must always learn anew to adapt his movement to his changing body if he does not want to become clumsy and awkward. And it is in back, where he cannot see, where he feels the most insecure because anything can attack him there, that his strength resides, the source of his power.

Everything is movement

Movement is the element of horses. Horses dance, mate, rejoice, and mourn with their bodies. Their spirit finds expression in movement. Movement is the culture, the music, the language, the life of horses.

How a horse feels is how he moves, and how he moves is how he feels.

Hard to believe! This horse has, for his whole life, moved stiffly and with far too much muscle contraction. Today, this now 20-year-old Arabian gelding shows himself off with elastic flowing movement, full of power. To achieve this "miracle" he did nothing for two years except to consciously get to know his own body, slowly, step-by-step on a circle in the arena. Here you see Passaro in piaffe, relaxed, at ease, on a loose line, "sitting" in high collection with deeply flexed haunches.

What Interests a Horse?

If we invite a horse to do something with us, he will soon pose the question, "Why, for what purpose, am I doing this?" Certainly we can give treats or praise or put some kind of reward in view. In the previous chapter, we saw that in a good relationship a horse is thoroughly willing to perform certain tasks merely for the sake of doing his person a favor. But, a horse is not like a dog who becomes wildly enthusiastic when he can satisfy his master. The horse will ask himself why we want this particular thing from him, and we should have an answer. Horses are different—and what makes a horse happy is also different.

We can bring our horse to a lush meadow where his friends are, or a few mares, if we are dealing with a stallion. Such an activity would make this horse happy and would immediately make sense to him. "Oh, that is why I was supposed to walk on this path. This was a good idea of yours!" But, we seldom behave this way. As a rule, the tasks required of a horse by human beings are less pleasant, strenuous to painful, and yes, even harmful to the horse. And they are almost always totally incomprehensible. If what we would like is genuine, freely given effort, we must explain and prove to him that he himself will benefit from the task. Then the thing suddenly becomes very interesting.

What interests a horse? What can I do that creates an advantage, a benefit for my horse—a benefit he would not have if he was alone and master of himself? Of course, I can lock my horse up for hours, days, or years so that he is overjoyed when he is actually allowed to move around a little bit. Movement is a basic need of horses, and if it is withheld, an emergency situation is created, similar to what would happen if we withheld food or water. The horse's urge to move builds up, he becomes explosive and is no longer careful of himself. The oppressive desolation of being confined is, in the long run, worse than the stress of riding. That is why horses kept in boxes or even tied in straight stalls are more "grateful" to be worked than horses living in a herd on pasture. The more the everyday life circumstances of a horse are improved, the less likely he is to unconditionally go along with whatever we have in mind.

A horse's happiness is different

So, if a horse has sufficient opportunity to move, if he can run and play at will—then what?

A horse feels at home on his feet. Safety through movement—from the first hours of his life a horse devotes himself to the art of movement.

For Example, Shane

The principle of "walking beautifully"

Last autumn young Shane once again succeeded in wrangling his way into the riding arena. I do not think it is good to regularly take young horses there, and would rather avoid it, even when they offer to go. But, Shane did manage it. For a few minutes we did something together. He felt good doing it, was very proud of himself, and moved the way a proud horse does. "You are moving great!" I told him. Through the whole winter this youngster remembered these few minutes, and often reminded me of them. When I let the colts and stallions out into their winter pasture, they usually just run past me. But, if Shane notices that I am looking at him in a certain way—and he often tries to get the message across to me that I should look at him (I do not quite know how he manages to do this)—he arches his neck and gravely, deliberately begins to move proudly. "Hey, look how great I can move!" It pleases him to capture my eye and make me marvel at him. It pleases him to impress me with his movement. It pleases him to move with such elevation. And I am pleased that Shane "speaks" to me in this manner.

Movement is so important to horses, such a central focus of living, that they interest themselves in it all their lives. More precisely, the quality of movement interests them. They are always ready to find new ways to improve it. How such improvement looks is something we will now study more closely.

Once this was...Max, going around a turn like a freighter overloaded in front. Such uneven loading during turns is very hard on the forelegs because of the sideways torque.

Once this was...Kim working on the circle. Here he has already begun to listen to his body. The severe contraction of his back muscles—a kind of protective shield against "everything up there"—does not allow his hind legs to step under any further yet. At that time, Kim was a very tight horse, whether or not he was being ridden.

Once this was...Passaro, the way he moved when we had been working together for several months. He is no longer fighting everything, nor is he tearing down the arena fencing anymore. Accordingly, the tension in his body has decreased. When it increases, he still explodes, but he really does not want to do that. For a long time Passaro just let himself fall on the forehand, lengthening and stretching the muscles that had hardened over the years. His weight is on his shoulders. This photo shows Passaro three years before the picture-perfect, deeply "sitting" piaffe in the photo on page 106.

The Transformation of Horses

When the relationship with human beings becomes helpful to horses, they can completely transform themselves during the course of work. Here we show you the beginning of work that may perhaps look similar to ordinary work on the longe line, but is actually taking place on a completely different level. It is not about the horse moving, but rather about the quality of the movement itself. The preceding three photos show the horses, Max, Kim, and Passaro during their first year of working with us. It is not the fact that a horse is going, but *how* he is going that is important to me in this work.

It is in a horse's nature to concern himself with the quality of his movement and to try to perfect it throughout his life. Can I, a human being who also spent years learning to walk, be useful to a horse in this respect?

Yes, I can. I have a number of abilities that a horse does not possess in the same form: the ability to analyze, the ability to concentrate on details, my goal orientation or the ability to think strategically, my individual kinesthetic sense along with my own experience

What a person can offer

with many forms of movement from crawling to walking upright. In addition there are the observations and ideas of other horses I have met. Instead of using these abilities to conquer and oppress my horse, I can offer them to him as support! What does that mean to the horses? Kim, the Haflinger whose muscles were so tight he could barely move from the spot—even when he wanted to—was offered a wide selection of exercises to choose from. The ones he preferred were endless voltes and a lot of shoulder-in. Through these exercises he alternately stretched both sides of his body so that he could then bring his hind legs further underneath himself. For the first time he got a sense of the power dormant within him.

With Passaro, on the other hand, a more therapeutic intervention was required. He needed a framework in which his aggressive outbursts were not blocked or further inflamed, and which gave him such a sense of security that he simply did not need the outbursts anymore. Because everything was allowed, he did not need to fight against anything. Then he worked for a long time with a very slack body tone, letting himself fall on the forehand as he dissolved tensions he had held for years. Often he slouched—occasionally also with a hanging lower lip—round and round the arena, looking outwardly very lazy, but inwardly in deep concentration and always ready to instantly attack if anything crossed him (for example, if he felt disturbed by a dopey expression on an onlooker's face).

How did Max do it? We met him a few pages ago at play and at work, and we shall see more of him.

Paths of development—Kim, Max, Passaro

The Anatomy of Movement

Before we occupy ourselves with the horse and his movement in detail, let us once more remind ourselves that this animal lived for millions of years in endless open spaces. If we compare a horse's body to ours, we notice several things: although the horse has so much more weight to carry than a human being, his legs are bonier and more delicate than ours. The muscles for the extremities are higher on the body. Like fingers—a human being's most used body part—horses' legs are stretched and directed by a network of tendons and ligaments. If you roll up your sleeve and look at your forearm as you move your fingers up and down, you will get an idea of what I mean. The horse has used this network very effectively. He touches the ground with only the tip of an elongated toe, and in doing so, balances on the tip of his middle "toenail." So, he can take long steps with a minimum expenditure of energy. This is a great advantage to an animal that must spend most of his day on his feet carrying his large body mass. Someone who has to move continually through the land in search of food while carrying a half-ton of body weight needs a system of movement that optimizes energy use so that expenditure does not become greater than the energy gained through the sustenance that is found.

The horse's toe, the human finger

Standing and moving on flat ground requires relatively little of the horse's power. A short pull of muscles yields maximum movement of the slender legs. Their movement is for the most part restricted to a forward and back swing. Knee and elbow joints have very little freedom as the tendons are, so to speak, tied to the body and swing from front to back. The horse's movement apparatus is intended for linear forward movement over vast, level expanses. A horse can cover long, flat, straight stretches of ground very economically. He is the perfect mover for this situation. Down to the tips of his toes, the horse is a specialist in conserving muscle energy while moving. He carries his body in a high, narrow, horizontal line and moves in high gear. As with a bicycle with large wheels, this kind of movement saves energy over long, level stretches. Horses are highly specialized creatures

Horse supervision—the horse, as teacher, shows us how it is done. He presents an authority that we hold in esteem and respectfully listen to. Reno always has the higher position and oversees everything with his kind eye.

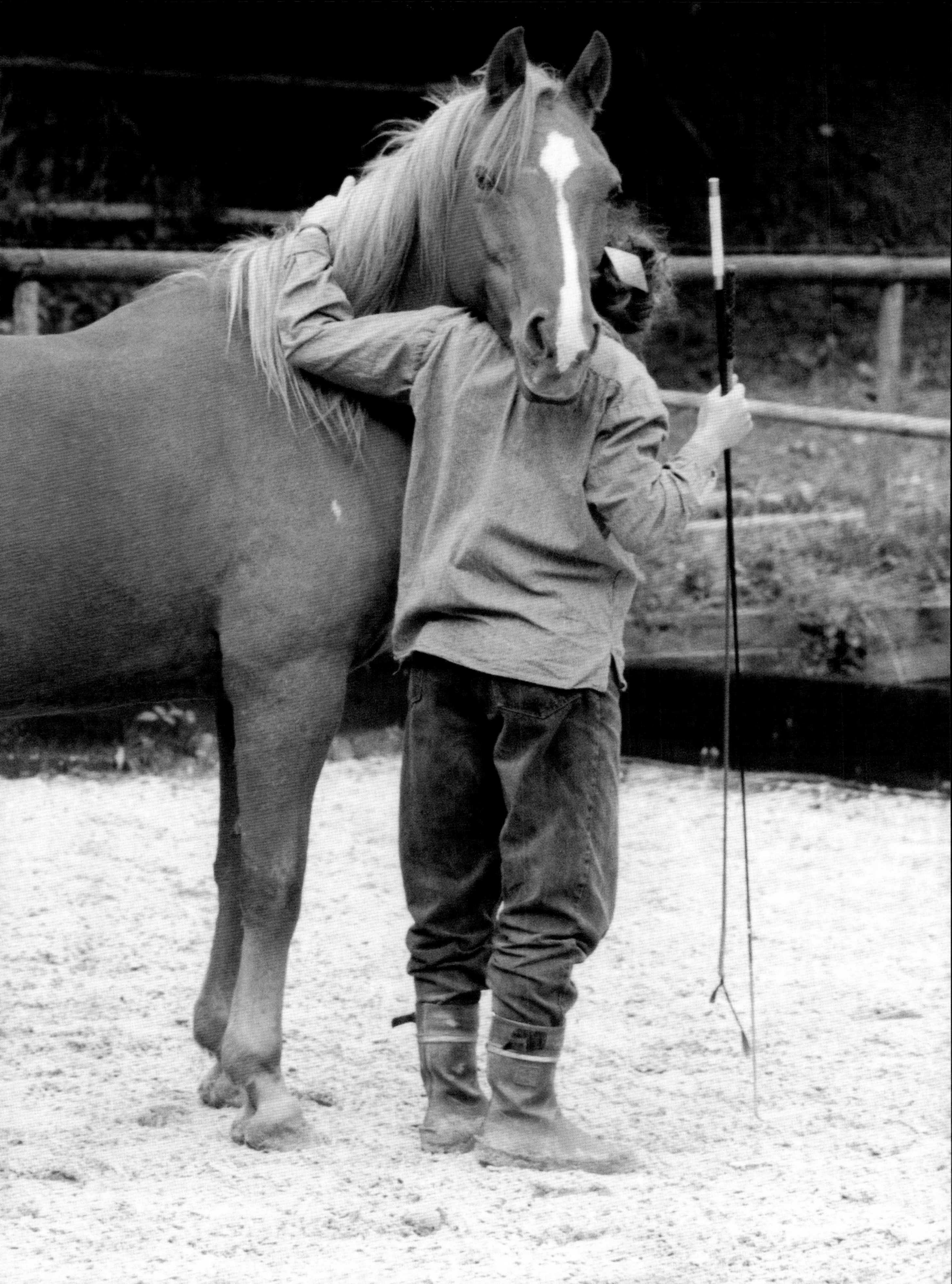

"Classical horsemanship flourishes only where the human being sees in the horse an equal."
~G. E. Löhneysen, 1609

of movement. But, it is precisely because they were created for movement that horses are susceptible to strains and injuries in this area, and very disturbed by restriction of movement. A horse that moves badly or with difficulty is not comfortable in his own skin.

The Problem with Training

The first steps

Having newly entered this world, a horse must maintain his balance and learn to walk, or he will not be able to take one sip of his mother's milk, and he will not survive for even one day. He does nothing in his early time as a foal but practice moving, again and again, at all speeds, under all circumstances. He lets no opportunity to develop his feel for movement, in every conceivable aspect, go by unused. This is necessary because he has an ever heavier body to balance high up off the ground on comparatively thin limbs, and as he grows, his balance changes constantly. His body weight increases nearly tenfold, his proportions shift continually. Sometimes the forelegs grow more rapidly, sometimes the hind legs. It is devastating when young horses are kept in stalls before they are fully grown. No wonder that, confined in such a small space, they cannot develop their feel for movement. Even if they were permitted to run and play as youngsters, their grown-up bodies are heavy and plump compared to then. Early riding work will drive whatever feel they developed as foals right out of them. No more carefree play, no experimenting with movement and experiences. Instead, there is external control and pressure to perform, and a person on his back who does not ask and does not care about the horse's feel for his body, but rather demands obedience.

The person who studies the horse and his movement will be confronted with highly complex interconnections of which we, as human beings, have barely any knowledge. A horse moves more beautifully without a human on his back. The demands are high on a trainer who seeks to change a horse's movement for the better. On the other hand, disrupting a horse's movement is easy. The mechanical "improvement" of a horse's movement is a hopeless undertaking, a task I can never fulfill. I need constant advice, corrections, directions, and confirmation that I am still on the right path. But, I am not alone in this undertaking. My horse is with me. And I am overjoyed that I can ask him, "What can I do, that will do you good?" "Which movement is better for you?" "How does that feel?" An independent horse sets a high standard for his human working partner because all the work will be measured by how helpful and useful its day-to-day effects are to the horse. Our horse expresses himself openly. He can say, "No, not like that!" He shows us clearly where we stand—we can no longer fool ourselves. But, that helps us, too. It is precisely this clarity that brings us onto the right path. A communicative horse like this is an irreplaceable and incorruptible teacher.

A communicative horse will express how he feels and show the way

In training a horse there is a huge grey zone, and there are many questions that a human cannot answer by himself. It is never entirely clear whether a horse has not understood something, or if he just does not want to do something, or if perhaps something hurts, which could ultimately damage him if he were to attempt the requested action. What separates the experienced from the inexperienced trainer is that the former has more knowledge and technique, but above all, that he operates with greater self-confidence in this grey area. Certainty, however, is something neither one has. The measures one takes prove to be inappropriate only in hindsight, and the consequence may only be apparent years later when the horse has changed owners several times. At that point, who still remembers exactly what went before? Individual horses are very different. The person who works with horses as equals has very communicative partners, who will always make very clear when and how something is wrong. That gives the trainer an immediate and certain course correction—the horse shows the way!

How Do I Actually Move?

Day after day, as though it were purely a matter of course, a person brings his body—which after all does weigh quite a bit—into movement hundreds of times. We get up in the morning, go to the window, walk down the stairs, sit on a chair, get up from it. How do we do this? Hardly any of us think about how we use our bodies. It has been a long time since we learned—only complete movement patterns are recalled.

Perhaps you have never had to pitch hay bales into a loft or needed to lift heavy bags of feed, but surely you have at some time needed to move a heavy cabinet or carried a case of beverages. Whether or not we injure our back while performing such tasks is largely a matter of technique. Results depend upon where the body is positioned relative to the object to be moved. Whether we walk or run, carry or pull, what counts is that the movement begins from the most advantageous point so that we do not needlessly exert ourselves nor incur too much bodily wear and tear. He who finds the right spot can lift the world off its axis. It is not just a matter of deploying strength but how I lift or carry something, where I lever and push that determines the amplitude of its movement. It is not enough simply to exert oneself—moving something large and heavy requires finding the right spot. Otherwise I just squander my energy, twist and strain my body, and perhaps even injure myself. To cause something heavy to become light and mobile we must go with the centers of gravity—our own and that of the other—and connect them both in the flow of directed energy.

The flow of energy

On the Balance of the Body

Someone who wants to keep his spine healthy lifts and carries from a point as close as possible to his body's center of gravity. Someone who has had problems with his knees will be careful not to place his legs at too much of an angle or too far from his center of gravity. He senses immediately how dangerous it can be when the joints are overburdened by muscle leverage placed at the wrong spot. Ouch! Maybe you too have had to struggle with such problems. That can now help you to understand the particularities of horses, because all these problems of center of gravity and balance, direction of movement and pushing power, are even greater for a horse. His body's center of gravity is much higher, his belly is significantly heavier, and the supports, his legs, which must carry everything, consist almost solely of thin bones, tendons, and ligaments, which means, they are not very flexible. And finally, a horse often moves very fast.

Center of gravity and balance

How he places his legs is significant for a horse, too. The quality and economy of his movement, the health of his body versus its premature wearing out, depend upon him placing his hooves on exactly the right spot. If the horse always finds this spot, his movement will be light and effortless. He will have more energy because his strength is not being squandered in a struggle with his own body weight. He can play with gravity—springing, leaping, and floating on air...

If a horse does not know this spot—perhaps because he was never able to experience it or because his feel for his body was damaged—his movement will be rough, inefficient, clumsy, and result in a great deal of wear and tear. No wonder that at some point moving will no longer be a pleasure. Moving like that is just a burden.

The power point

Together with our horses we work to find this magic spot, the point of power—the

"How do you deal with the bend?" This seemingly harmless question separates the wheat from the chaff in the world of horsemanship. The young Connemara mare, Hazel, is shown here at the beginning of her training. Although she, too, is turning on her inside foreleg as Max was on page 108, Hazel is also trying to bring her hindquarters along. To do that, she stretches her inner hind leg far underneath her body. Although this makes the turn somewhat easier, her body as a whole is leaning at an angle, like a motorcycle does when its rider leans in around a curve. In this position, a horse could easily fall and his legs are put under great stress.

In this photo, Hazel is no longer making the turn like a motorcycle, but rather, more like an articulated truck: she is turning by bending the middle of her body to a greater degree. In both these ways of dealing with the bend, the axis of Hazel's turn is just behind her left shoulder, the place where her natural center of gravity is. Behind us, Joy is waiting her turn. She will soon show us how she deals with the bend.

right point relative to the body for precisely this movement, for precisely this body in this particular position. If we are successful and we find this spot, we can, together, lift the world off its axis. The horse's enormous weight hardly matters anymore, nor does the added weight of a rider. Finding the magic spot—that is the secret of horsemanship; that is the secret of dancing horses.

The Leaping-Off Point

What horseman does not want to give his horse wings so that his movement is light and flowing? The search for the point where the horse's heaviness dissolves presents three problems. The horse is not static! He is constantly moving and by doing so, he changes his posture, which changes the location of the point. To find the horse's "point of lightness" I need to educate my eye regarding his movement, but that does not decide it because the whereabouts of the horse's center of gravity depends on his emotional state, too. For example, a horse that has been startled, has his point moved forward immediately. He falls onto the forehand. So, to determine the center of gravity, it is also important to know how the horse feels in that moment. The third problem is, how can I then let the horse know where the point is and how can I persuade him to put his foot where it needs to be? No wonder a horseman can spend his whole life on this. But today, the place where many riders are seeking the point of lightness—in the horse's mouth—is surely where it is not! The mouth is never the point of lightness! To have it so, the horse would need to do a headstand.

Getting to "the point"

Is the horse's center of gravity in his mind?

We too will now join the search. So that we do not wander too far off course, we will make things easier on ourselves. We will ask the horses about the subject as we go round in a circle for a bit.

The Horse in the Turn

Every day countless horses go round and round in circles: in riding arenas, round pens, longeing circles, making large circles, voltes, and always the corners. What actually takes place when a horse turns, changes direction? How does he feel as he does it? How does it feel to move with four legs on a curved line? It seems so matter-of-fact because in our restricted world a horse must constantly go around a bend. But it is not so! Let us make a few rounds with the horses so that we can better understand it.

Today, in the custody of human beings, the horse moves only from corner to corner, but he is an animal made to move on long, straight, level stretches. On the firm grass steppes he moved steadily and efficiently, and occasionally very fast. But, the physique of such a "distance mover" is not supposed to make a lightning-quick sprint and attack like a feline predator, nor can it slink quickly around trees or glide through the underbrush like a rabbit. The predisposition of horses to move in a straight line is reflected in their body structure, and also in their psyche. A roaming horse sees something off in the distance and either heads straight toward it, or avoids it by putting more distance between it and himself. Young, relaxed horses, who move with their neck long and low, reveal to their rider where they will go next by always "following their noses" and going toward where they are looking. If something off to the side gets their attention, they will stop, because looking off to the side while moving forward goes against a horse's nature. The more excited a horse is, the more his natural inclination to move in a straight line comes into play—many a person has shaken his head at the crazy creature that cannot find the way round something and instead crashes mindlessly through the hedge or fence just to get to the other side.

A linear animal

JOY'S PATH TO THE BEND: PART 1—Joy is more of a "stretched" horse with the long lines desirable in a broodmare. On her own, she moves through a turn like a ship, and on her forehand. Here we are trying to shift the "turning point" of the movement somewhat further back, to where the rider's leg is. Even if a horse is still moving like a wheelbarrow, the reins should not turn him. The turn should happen from behind! Here, the inside rein is hanging slack while the outside one is serving to create a boundary to help her bring that outside shoulder along in the turn, rather than getting it stuck in place.

Horses originate in wide open spaces where no "going around things" is necessary; rather, the shortest, most direct way is what counts. Their thinking is not wound in circles. Without question, the most decisively linear act is flight. Stampeding horses run nearly blindly straight ahead. They run as though fleeing from a prairie fire, and in today's world that horses now inhabit, this can be very dangerous. Horses can be so caught up in their "linearity" that they crash into obstacles rather than trying to avoid them. Horrible accidents have happened because of this tendency. But in the world they came from, this linear behavior was very sensible. In that place, turns at high speed were unnecessary as well as risky because they put great stress on the tendon and ligament network of the horse's slender legs.

Let's get out of here!

Is every turn, therefore, potentially dangerous to a moving horse? Fundamentally, yes—but there are exceptions: when playing and "fighting," horses turn and bend their bodies even at high speed. Of course, they are in command of a very different body balance than normal—a balance that is centered closer to their hind legs than usual. We can compare a horse's normal balance while grazing or walking leisurely to a wheelbarrow, but one with two front wheels set apart. The "push" comes from behind and the weight is held and supported in front. This normal balance of the horse is shifted further backward during the welling-up of emotion that occurs during play and attack. What this displacement toward the haunches affects and how it increases mobility is something we can easily try out for ourselves if we get down on all fours.

That special balance

On Bending and Breaking

A horse that takes more weight onto his hindquarters becomes much more mobile and can easily change direction. This shift of balance, however, requires great effort, just as if a person were to move with deeply bent knees. Such an expenditure of energy would, of course, be the last thing on a horse's mind when he is stressed and insecure during work. But, as long as he supports the majority of his weight on his forehand and occasionally pushes from behind, circles and turns are a danger to his legs. If you love your young horse, therefore, you should avoid longeing him at the beginning of training to protect him from injury. Most young horses, because of their balance, are not able to turn safely with a rider on their back. Nevertheless, turning is what is practiced over and over again in order to "bend" the horse. But a horse does not become more supple through forced bending or by turns executed when he is stiff. On the contrary! In fact, when moving through turns in this manner becomes habitual, the horse will become increasingly stiffer and heavier, and his movement progressively deteriorates as he compensates and tries to protect himself from injury. The wheelbarrow swings around the turn with the weight in front, the hindquarters drift to the outside...and the very "clever" rider presses his horse into the corner—into bending and breaking! The more on his forehand a horse is when the rider does this the greater the likelihood of him being damaged by these forceful methods.

Going through the turn on stilts?

Please do not bend!

A horse cannot be "bent" by external means. Bending—if by that one does not mean a "broken" neck or an otherwise disconnected horse—cannot be forced! Because of this fact some people contend that regular, even, longitudinal bending of a horse's body is anatomically impossible, but this is not true. However, it is not possible to achieve it by external means. The horse's body cannot be forcefully bent by human hands: broken, yes; bent, no. A horse must learn for himself how to arrange his body in this position. Whoever seeks to produce bend by mechanical means will never know the real thing. It is shocking that today we hardly ever see a horse that can move correctly through the curve. It is a good test of serious training to ask: "How do you deal with the corner?" What the horseman

The turn signals the direction

In these photos, we are much closer. My aids are being accepted as such, that is, as a helpful "prompting." Toppur is concentrating deeply on his own body, he is less concerned about me. Now, I can energetically support him "stepping under" with the hind leg since he will accept my support as he needs it. In the bottom photo, notice the effort he is making to place his legs so that they are in line—this makes him stronger and more mobile. By doing so, he comes closer to his "magic point" than if he were placing his feet to the outside, legs apart.

The working distance between us decreases a bit more and Toppur tries the whole thing at a trot. He himself had already increased the degree of difficulty by making the circle smaller. Now he is trying to make the smaller circle at a faster gait: what an ambitious athlete! Even for an outsider it is easy to see that the horse is becoming more and more goal-oriented as he finds his own way. It is Toppur who is driving this process forward. I accompany and support him, but he is the proactive party. Also, it's very interesting to see a completely different aspect of this horse's development: during the few minutes in the arena, his whole presence has changed. In the beginning, he looked rather youthfully naïve, but during the work his self-possession clearly increases. He collects, becomes more upright, feels more certain of himself. He steps into another dimension and seems larger, more majestic—more empowered.

How correct movement comes to be

to do this. The photos of the Connemara mares, Hazel and Joy, which accompany the text, show different stages of the learning process. The first issue is the horizontal bend, and a horse can only learn this when he understands that he should embrace the rider's aids rather than avoid them, that is, come "toward" the aids rather than moving away from them. That way he can bend around a whip or a leg, accept the bit rather than avoid it, and round his back to "meet" the rider's weight. But, we do not want to reach into the next chapter just yet.

For now we will have a look at Toppur to see how he deals with the problem of the curved line. At first there are tiny, perhaps barely visible changes that occur during the work. But a horse that is schooled, worked, and motivated in this positive manner will soon find his correct posture, as if on his own.

The Third Dimension

A horse that learns to bend himself and more consciously and precisely place his legs will move more economically and also just look more beautiful. The horse will make a different impression: we just saw how the Icelandic stallion went through a transformation on the circle that greatly changed the presence he radiated. What made that happen—and in such a short time? Is Toppur simply proud of his great achievement? Is that why he seems larger, more impressive, more majestic? Certainly quality of movement has aftereffects on a horse's psyche and we will explore this reciprocal influence further. But, the horse's increased growth in height and the impressive picture he presents have a very real physical cause. This is the third dimension of movement. We can move in a straight line—that is the first dimension. And we can move on a curved line and back and forth across the landscape—the second dimension. In addition, we can move a bit more "upward" by carrying ourselves in an upright posture. This "growth" through upright carriage is one of the most important principles of horsemanship and has been the source of much confusion. With the help of the horses we will now try to find our way into the third dimension.

The path upward

How many methods have riders devised to get their horses into an upright, elevated carriage? From check reins that run over the neck to hold up the horse's head, to raising the hand to elevate the horse's neck and head, to artificial "riders," also known as "dumb jockeys"—all sorts of tricks have been tried to elevate the horse's forehand. Most of them are pure torture. For very simple reasons it is impossible to do what people try to do with these devices. Just as Baron von Munchausen could not pull himself out of the swamp by his own pigtail, you cannot force a horse into elevated carriage. All you can do is yank his head and neck up. The desired growth of the horse cannot be manipulated—it needs to evolve from appropriate schooling of the whole horse. This so-called "passive" lightening of the forehand cannot be not actively "produced," it arises as a "side effect" when the horse begins to move in a certain manner. As he does, he does not grow "taller" in front; he actually gets "shorter" behind as he flexes the joints in his haunches. Kim, Hazel, and Joy will shed further light on how this happens. They learned it in the turn.

What does an "upright frame" mean here?

When a horse moves on a curved line, his hind legs have more room to step further forward because the individual hind hoof does not follow the corresponding front foot as when going straight but rather, heads diagonally underneath the middle of the horse's body. So there is no danger of the horse stepping on his own feet from behind, which often happens to awkward horses when their natural flow of movement is thrown off its habitual equilibrium, either by the rider or because of the way the horses are shod. The horse in a longitudinal bend does not need to take shorter steps, rather he can reach as far forward as possible without worrying about his forelegs. He can first try out the movement with his hind leg without worrying about whether he will get the forefoot out of the way quickly

Practice curves—free space for the hind leg

Here is the Haflinger gelding, Kim, in the turn. His body is nicely, evenly bent. The origin and center of the movement is the inside hind leg. The left side of his body is light and free, the hindquarters are reaching far forward toward the center of gravity.

Hazel is stepping far forward under her body with her right hind leg. At the same time, she is tipping her sacrum down and lowering one hip. Through this movement the inside hind leg exerts a pull that goes diagonally over the stretched back muscles to the horse's outside forehand, which in turn becomes lighter and higher. Hazel assumes an elevated posture with the impetus from behind. She becomes "taller in the turn."

enough. That way he can create a secure base for himself. In the top photo on page 127, Kim puts his left hind leg far under his body. In doing so, he will put weight on this leg longer, and briefly also more heavily than on the outside hind leg. With this one-sided reach more forward, he will also move his croup differently, tilt his pelvis a bit forward, and use the left hindquarter to come even further forward under the center of gravity.

The "Right Twist"

What happens when a horse tries to bring the spot where he places his hind feet and his center of gravity closer to one another, while he is also shifting his center of gravity further back, as Hazel just did?

If you would like to try for yourself how this feels, lay your right leg on an ottoman or the edge of a sofa and reach for your right toes with your left hand. This is the kind of stretch a horse feels. And it increases when you add weight and shift further backward. So, in the turn the horse performs a kind of stretch and bends the hip on one side. The stretch pulls diagonally over the back. Now the horse seems more three-dimensionally bent, or "turned into" himself. After all, the spine is not like a rigid "rod" but rather a multi-jointed one that can move in all directions. For human beings, that means that we not only can bend our bodies forward, backward, and from side to side, but that shoulders and hips can be "twisted" counter to one another. The pure horizontal bend of a horse feels something like this: stand straight and let your arms hang at your side. Now try to lengthen one arm toward the floor. Your body will bend to that side, and will get stretched on the other. You will also respond with this motion if someone pokes you in the side, like a horse "yielding" to the spur. What we see with the horses here, though, has an additional element. It is similar to what you feel if you try the following exercise. With your right leg on a small footstool or stair step, turn a bit to the right as if you were going to walk up a spiral staircase. "Upward, forward, sideways instead of forward, sideways," that is how the movement goes. This can be easily seen in the eight photos of Toppur in the photo series that started on page 122. And in a previous photo series ("Joy's Path to the Bend: Part 3," on page 121) even Joy is already showing a tendency to become more upright. Because these horses are bending from within themselves and turn from behind, they will, as a matter of course, get the "right twist." Joy's photos on page 129 make this very clear.

We walk up a spiral staircase

Hazel just showed us how she finds the right point from which to bring her whole body into an elevated frame from behind. When horses lower the inside hip and move the center of gravity backward, they can turn more comfortably and in a more centered way than they can from a solely horizontal bend. Even in extremely tight turns their legs will not be subject to torque, that is, weighted unevenly at an angle. This posture is much more advantageous for the horse when he encounters centrifugal forces in the turn and he learns to absorb them lightly and with elasticity. Whether a horse intentionally places his feet can be seen by the hoof prints he leaves. Our horses do not leave furrows or deep prints off the edges of the track in the corners. Only after guest horses have used the arena do we sometimes need to smooth out the footing.

In rigid crookedness or with a light, elastic step?

Joy too has now found the "right twist" and she discovers how quickly and handily she suddenly can turn if she shifts her body weight to the inside hind leg (bottom photo on page 129). She turned left so quickly that I am surprised by the swiftness of her movement and my upper body is left a bit behind the motion. Can you see this? Joy actually did take me along in the movement but she had not taken into account that, because I sit so high up, I accelerate more slowly—and later—than she does.

Notice on page 129 that Joy reduced the size of her base of support in order to make the

An upward movement has originated from the longitudinal bend. Joy has found the "magic spot," which makes it easy for her to change direction even with a rider. This is how horses turn when they have found the "right twist."

Joy now wants to know: "How fast can I turn when I do it this way?" With deeply bent hind legs placed far underneath her body, she turns powerfully and close to her center of gravity. In a few weeks the once almost ponderous Joy has transformed herself into a lightning-quick powerhouse.

How Bending Leads to Collection—Five Steps to Passage

Here the horse uses his movement through the corner to increase his collection to such an extent that he is able to effortlessly find his way into a more elevated movement. Let's examine exactly how Passaro does this.

In the series of photos here, first we see him in a nice collected frame as he trots dynamically and rhythmically toward the corner. In the next step, he prepares himself for the corner by making the hind-quarters even more active and reaching far underneath himself. The energy flows through his body, already preparing for the corner with a slight bend, unhindered from the tip of his tail to the tip of his nose. In the third photo, because of too much push from the right hindquarter, Passaro finds himself too linear for the curve on which he is traveling. We both notice it. So, Passaro rounds his body and adjusts it once more to the curved line by placing his right hind leg even further toward the center of his body. Because of that, this leg bears more weight and Passaro uses the moment to transform his powerfully rhythmic trot action into high collection (pushing power into carrying power) and as he comes out of the corner he begins to passage.

turn, and in doing so she made herself more mobile, like an ice skater doing the pirouette. To do this she deeply flexed her haunches, pushed them far underneath herself, and at the same time raised the forehand and became more upright. Her forelegs are hardly weighted at all, and the left hoof is so unburdened that the toe barely touches the ground. Despite Joy's speed, they are not being subjected to torque at all. Even though Joy is turning practically on the spot, she placed her legs straight under her body and absorbed the momentum in the same place she developed it: with the excellent dynamic of her elastic, springy haunches.

Whirling on tiptoe—the elasticity of the hindquarters

The Magical Circle

The foundation for sensible and successful transformation of horses is the desire and will of the individual animal to improve himself and his movement. But he will only want to do this in a safe environment. And in the process, he wants to be consulted and permitted to express his views, because ultimately the subject in question is the central concern of his life. He would like to unfold himself, not be forcibly changed from the outside, because in addition to the danger such external manipulation poses to the horse with his very sensitive system of movement based on an unstable equilibrium, forced exercises also entail a massive loss of personal freedom.

An "unfolding" of self rather than a forced posture

Horses do not resist changing—they resist being changed by external means. The best motivation to change, for horses as for people, is one's own desire.

That may sound very abstract to someone familiar only with the principle of "drive or be driven." But, as soon as the chemistry is good between me and my horse, all sorts of small changes begin to occur—at first, perhaps very insignificant, even incidental. The horses themselves initiate the process, hesitantly, on a "trial basis."

On a foundation of freedom horses transform themselves very quickly. With an incredibly powerful dynamic they breeze through various levels of training and, on their own, practice what they have learned. That is why such work is uncommonly effective and is retained even after long periods of not working. After all, the horse knows the way because he himself has blazed the path. He regularly seeks your aids—he actually uses the human like a personal trainer! It is a remarkably different and very moving feeling to ride like this.

The human being is useful

The Power of Transformation

The nicest thing about this work is that we finally have a pure, incorruptible standard for evaluating the quality of our actions: our horse's approval. His enthusiasm grows, he becomes more and more madly eager to move, to collect, he takes over the arena—all showing me that my work cannot be so very wrong! And in case of illness or injury, who can tell me better than my horse himself what work is sensible and helpful, and what is painful or potentially injurious? I experienced this with Reno, who several years ago could barely move anymore. With great effort he managed to limp to the water trough. Pain killers no longer helped him much. The vet thought perhaps a neurectomy, the removal of a nerve, might help, but could Reno manage our steep mountain pastures with no sensation in his feet? Up to that time, Reno had been a field, woods, and pasture horse with no interest in arena work, but suddenly he discovered the concept! He learned collection. He lightened his forehand. Today he initiates exercises like piaffe, pirouettes, and levade in order to bring his weight onto his haunches. He is unstoppable. Twenty-two years old and incurably lame he is now practicing the crowning achievement of haute école: capriole! You only have to see how commandingly he pushes his way into the arena—on some days wretch-

Reno and haute école

edly lame—how he gathers his assistants to help him, and how he does not leave the arena until he is satisfied with himself. We all stand there in utter amazement. I was in no way an expert in these things. All I did, a long time ago, was to help this horse understand a concept. From then on, he has explained everything to me.

When a rider practices bending, turning, and moving on a circle in an arena in order to improve the horse's movement, it is called "dressage." In common usage the concept "dressage" has come to mean the mindless and soulless execution of proscribed movements. That sort of dressage is mere form, empty of substance. Unfortunately, horse training usually proves this characterization correct. The horse has no opportunity to understand what he is doing, and takes no part in the movement. Sadly, this sort of horse training still means the mechanization of the horse for the rider's benefit: the goal is simply to make the horse function more smoothly with nary a hitch. Today, for some reason, many riders want to contribute to the betterment of their horses, and that is a particular argument used in favor of classical horsemanship. Some people are even convinced that horses can only arrive at their true self-expression through this kind of "shaping" by the rider.

And where does this leave the horse?

True, there is powerful potential for transformation through classical horsemanship. But, how can a horse grasp the true intent, if the rider himself does not know it, if every hoofprint pattern, every exercise that he accomplishes against the horse's opposition is apparently closer to his heart than the horse himself? Any art form—so it seems to me—is unthinkable without freedom, spontaneity, and individuality. Movement art must be something more than automated steps, postures, and gestures one after another.

And where is the "Art"?

Bringing animals into a certain "artistic" shape and holding them there through barely visible threads of command and control is still just a variation of common mechanical dressage. Art can only exist where there is space for inspiration, a variety of creative possibilities, and spontaneous joy in the doing. Art with horses does not have to be a puppet theater. It can be art for the horse's well-being.

There are certain sequences of movement that can truly help horses to further develop their bodies and themselves. The conscious experience of his own physicality affects a horse's psyche as well; it allows him to become more self-possessed and empowered. As his self-image improves and his trust in himself grows, he will further improve physically—a process I find incredibly exciting. You will hear more about this in the next chapter.

Meanwhile, Toppur has learned not only how to keep his balance on a circle, but how to use the circle for further development and perfection. The result is spectacular! Wonderfully balanced and with perfect concentration, Toppur leaps into what is nearly a Baroque gallopade: movement art!

"I have never put up resistance...I felt that I did not have the right to change another if I myself was not open to being changed by him."

~Martin Buber

On the Art of Transformation

Emotion—Feelings in Motion

Have you ever wept for joy, or shivered with excitement even though you were not the least bit cold? Perhaps you know the feeling of being paralyzed by fear: you feel numb, as if your body no longer belongs to you. You move woodenly, rigidly, and are uncoordinated in all that you do. The simplest grab for an object can miss its mark because you are under such pressure. Every task is made more difficult, not easier, if it is associated with fear. Fear and anxieties cripple energy, stiffen the body and restrict movement like lead weights.

Our emotional life is reflected in our body, in its posture and its movement. When we overcome a difficulty, a heavy weight is lifted off our shoulders and we breathe deeply because an emotional burden has been removed. We feel light, as though we have sprouted wings—suddenly everything seems easy. Emotion—movement is even there as part of the very word. What moves us is directly connected to the way we move. The inner life affects the external image. A person swells with pride, and moves as though walking on air. But, how is it with animals? A horse, too, will move in an elevated posture if he feels strong, light, and proud. He suddenly looks as though he has grown. Animals are even closer to their emotions than we human beings are. For horses too, feelings and movement are inextricably connected, and inner balance finds its outer expression in the body. How a horse moves is how he feels, and how he feels is how he moves.

A moving feeling

If we want to change something about a horse, we should always remain aware of this special connection between movement and feelings. A horse can never truly change in his body if it is not possible for him to change his inner life to match. It is very important to consciously realize this. We shall come to see how this subject of feelings pertains to specific situations and how it affects our work. Who better to introduce us to this subject than the horses themselves? So, we shall begin with them. We'll ask them. Let's ask Max, because no one can show us as clearly as he can that feelings and quality of movement are one.

The oneness of body and spirit

We Called Him "Thunderclap"

The first time I met "the Maxi," he had just, once again, worked his way through the fence to snatch a few green blades of grass. That was his name then—Maxi. He was a small, flabby pony, tied to a fruit tree. Even so, he could push his way through the fence boards.

Max—what I remember most of all are his eyes. They were full of sorrow and hidden behind a thick forelock of wiry black hair. The little bay gelding did not look at me. His only interest was in what was edible, and like a bulldozer he barged toward it. Other things did not interest him at all.

But wait, there was one thing: Max did not want to be left alone or go somewhere alone. He was terribly attached to other horses. He began to sweat as soon as his halter was put on and he was to be led away, or when he thought or believed that he would be separated from the herd. Only in the group did he feel safely concealed. Out of fear of being alone he would, if necessary, barrel through fences and people. Even the chain over his nose could no longer contain such power. Fear aroused unexpected energy in this massive little guy. Whoever did not jump out of his way was trampled. Was he just a rude, fat lout? No, he was a frightened little horse whose big heart was buried under masses of fat—it was inaccessible even to him. Max screened himself off. To him it was all the same that he was not particularly noticed. After all, he himself paid attention only to eating. In

Strong, free, and in total concentration, Toppur appreciates my mental support but other than that he needs no aids from me to perform such a powerful, elevated canter. He knows the power point from which to leap—the two of us worked on the circle to collect his strength.

reality he was furious at, and disappointed in human beings. But such feelings are dangerous, so he swallowed them, internalized them as he "ate" them. Max remained a "nice guy" if perhaps a bit unshapely—a pony, in fact.

Max came to us. I began to work with him and he made every effort. He learned eagerly and was happy with any bit of praise (particularly in edible form). He thawed a bit and would reveal himself more often, and happily. He was a childlike gelding, perhaps even a bit socially retarded. Compared to the other horses he behaved like an uncertain yearling. Despite his advanced age, he still showed the submissive mouthing behavior of a foal, using that gesture to get the herd to spare and protect him. In our work together his entire way of going changed, and thanks to shoulder-in, Max soon was not tottering along as wide-legged as before. Despite his willingness, the training reached a limit—a natural one, by all appearances. There simply was no more to be had from this extremely front-heavy body. This pony with his bullish, overbuilt shape, short legs, stiff, fat-pocked neck, and massive heavy shoulders, was well designed to pull a plow, but why torture him with tasks for which he was clearly not intended, at which he could only fail? We worked our way up to a small travers at walk and decided to spare ourselves further effort.

Then, one day I saw Max run up to a strange dog trespassing in the pasture. Max struck out and stamped impressively with a foreleg and chased off the intruder in short order. I had not credited this shy gelding with such fighting spirit! Shortly after this incident, I had an inspiration while we were in the indoor arena: I kicked the riding boards that lined the wall and challenged Max to do the same. I enticed him with treats, took his leg and knocked it against the wood. At first he did not dare to do it, he gingerly put his foot against the board and I enthusiastically urged him on. As he made the first noise, he pulled back expecting an angry response. I reassured him and kicked the board hard myself so that it banged loudly and shook. It did not take long until Max was forcefully banging the riding boards with his front hoof. This created a huge racket. Max enjoyed the booming noise at full volume and could not get enough of it. I moved Max away from the boards. He understood that it was about the movement, and so became enchanted with the powerful gesture rather than the noise.

So far, so good. But suddenly little Max became difficult. He had discovered a powerful weapon: his own body. He felt strong, and sour toward the whole world. If he felt that he was being pressured, pushed or pulled, he attacked immediately. He could jump toward me diagonally through the longeing circle, strike out in front, and stomp aggressively in my direction. Max had even mastered the double-barreled strike with both forelegs. As he did this he seemed to radiate the sentiment: "No one will ever pressure me again. If someone tries, I'll flatten him!" On the other hand, he demanded to work with me. He crashed through the fencing and turned up in the arena, usually while another horse was concentrating on his work. "Now it's my turn. Right now!" So I had no alternative but to appease him. It was an unusual time. Max slouched along beside me steaming with sullenness, and every few steps he demanded a treat as tribute. How did we survive this period? We survived because I did everything that Max wanted. Though I was sweating in fear, I stuffed him full of treats, telling him how impressive he was and asking him if, yet one more time, he might graciously let me live. I scrupulously avoided anything that might suggest even the appearance that I was trying to establish any sort of dominance over him. Only a clicking of the tongue escaped from me now and then (usually involuntarily), for which I immediately had to apologize.

During this whole phase I did nothing to oppose or "correct" this horse, rather I did what was in my power to support, appease, and reinforce him. During our "conversations" in the arena, I served, soothed and admired Max. He intimidated and "mugged" me. But I

A small horse with grand gestures: Maximilian Thunderclap in the arena back then.

knew that he knew that I knew. We acted "as if"—yet at the same time, it was a very serious situation for both of us. After quite some time of expressing his rage, attacking every perceived "enemy" by striking out with his forelegs, Max reverted to conscious enjoyment of the pure movement, his anger now replaced with a regal calm.

Today, his rhythm and pushing power can barely be contained. Max is certain of himself, conscious of his own power, and he shows a high degree of self-confidence. His Spanish walk has great amplitude, his shoulder is light, he knows to "sit" on his haunches. Max broke through his limitations and left them far behind. He completely transformed himself. This new horse's movement is supple and magnificent, full of pride and dignity. "It feels as though a colossal whale is flying," is what one of his students once respectfully said when she was permitted to ride him. Max knows that he has conquered himself. And Max knows how to impress. When Maximilian Thunderclap—that is his fighting name—enters the arena, all conversation must stop. Mighty Max draws all attention to himself. His powerful radiance holds every onlooker spellbound.

Habitual Movement—Familiar Feelings

Everything as usual

When we begin work with a horse he has already been moving a certain way for years. Now a human being comes along and wants to change this habitual movement. Even though the manner in which a horse moves, turns, and carries himself is not determined entirely by anatomy, we know from our own experience how difficult it is to change habits with which we have lived for years. Even when we are aware of a better alternative and we ourselves want to change a particular faulty posture, we often do not stick with it very long because old patterns are stronger than even the best intentions. Ultimately, it is not what we do occasionally that counts but rather, what we de normally—and in that we unconsciously stay with the old pattern. After all, that is how it has always been the most comfortable. So, the new is soon done in the old way. Taking a course in a new way of moving does not, in and of itself, simply switch off everyday habits of movement. Rather, these old habits usually become more entrenched in response to the first efforts to change them. It is very seldom that we humans actually succeed in finding new, alternative ways of moving, even when we are shown them. And yet, that should be doable for a horse, even though we are ostensibly so much more conscious?! Can horses truly arrive independently at a new way of moving, or must they constantly be held in the new posture so that they do not fall back into old habits? Doesn't the rider have to continually see to it that the horse does not lose his position and come out of the desired posture—"fall apart," as the saying goes?

How they once were...

If you turn back to the photos of the beginning years of Passaro, Kim, and Max on pages 108 and 109, you can compare those early photos to the later ones of these horses throughout the book. It is not only the outer posture that is completely different! There is Passaro, still in those days a captive of his past, indefatigable in his flight, just beginning to acknowledge to himself that he is tired, exhausted from continually fighting. There is Kim with his slightly confused expression, a sometimes violent horse, though unintentionally so, who never felt quite grown-up in the world although, according to his age, he should have matured long ago. And there is Max, the fat little barrel of a pony, also introverted, always bound to the earth and trying only to be weightier, more massive. The horses in those photos live in their own worlds, their expression is rather unexpressive, and does not say much. They seem to be not very communicative. Do you get that impression from these early photos, compared to the ones taken at a later date? Can you see the differences?

The Body Does Not Lie

Every body position, every posture, has its own energy, makes its very own special statement. There is someone who goes through life upright, with an aware, open spirit, and he moves freely, lithely, in the flow of elastic power. He encounters a new situation with curiosity and is happy at the opportunity to learn. How different from one who is mistrustful, depressed, stagnant and blocked. His movement is agitated as though anticipating disaster. His behavior toward anything new is inflexible and fearful. His posture is rigid, hunched over, as though the attack he fears were already a physical reality. So, mental attitude very broadly determines posture, and fluctuations in mood are directly reflected in how a body moves and the quality of energy of those movements. A person's inner "posture" and his external one create one unified image, like the two sides of a coin they are inseparably connected to one another.

Emotion reveals itself in movement. That is a problem with learned-by-rote body language maneuvers as they are taught in clinics. If the gesture is not connected with genuine perception and feeling it will generate incongruity and that will be perceived as such by an aware counterpart. "Beware of him whose belly does not move when he laughs" warns a Chinese adage. The supposedly surefire selling techniques taught to sales reps are another example of such laid-on gestures. Even a sensitive person will not be won over by such an approach because he can sense the inconsistency—so certainly a horse will! When the taught behavior is not authentic, our subconscious registers this and transmits the message that something is amiss. An uncomfortable feeling is then associated with this person. He does not say what he is really thinking. He is smiling and speaking friendly words but...depending on the person we are speaking to, such disharmony can have a quite sinister effect. An image of confusion, dishonesty, and deception is created by these mixed messages. "What does he really want?" I nervously ask myself. At any rate, trust cannot exist when a person tries to conceal or downplay his real intentions. He spreads disharmonious energy, because inner and outer are not in agreement.

Dissonant body language

To Pride through Force?

Horses absolutely know when we human beings speak with a "forked tongue." And they are alarmed by it because the hunter sneaking up on them also tries to hide as much as possible his real intent with his body language, and to appear harmless. A discrepancy between inner and outer creates uneasiness in our counterpart and at the same time, in ourselves.

To be congruent, at one with self, is a condition with which not many people are familiar anymore. Often we are not even aware of our disharmony, but its effect—particularly on horses—is very negative. At the same time, we thoughtlessly demand this same sort of disharmony from our horses and try to force them into a similarly divided life. But a horse draws the majority of his power from the unbroken unity between expression and perception. In the language of horses a particular gesture makes a particular statement. Moving in a certain manner is the direct expression of the experience of the moment. Every movement is a feeling! The horse cannot move proudly if he does not feel proud! Movement is the message. When a horse learns higher level exercises under a rider he is expected to carry himself and move as though he were a self-confident stallion. But, think of a person in a straight jacket—he can never begin to dance loosely and happily or move impressively! Yet that is exactly what some riders demand. They try to force proud bearing onto a horse, often with great violence. Whatever is achieved that way is just an empty gesture, a "dance" of a marionette, a depressing illusion...a creature wrought by human power for the pleasure of spectators who are also human.

Dance, horse! But to my tune!

Sublime emotions, however, give wings to human and horse alike! When a horse feels noble, proud, and impressive he will gladly take on the elevated "form" and fill it with life and expression. But if we force the horse into a posture that he cannot bring into congruence and harmony with his emotional state, we create a dead language that estranges the horse from his body. We force him to renounce oneness with himself and drive him out of his body as though from a conquered land. The horse must sever himself from his movement and thereby give up his primal means of expression. He becomes "speechless," awkward, and powerless. Is there a way to respect and guard the horse's bodily integrity and yet change it?

The estranged horse

Shannon and the Saddle

Shannon, too, now wants to come to the riding arena, but he does not quite know what is going on when this woman suddenly tries to play with him. He participates—but hesitantly. Kirsten is obviously not a horse, so Shannon cannot simply have a carefree romp as with his horse buddies. Even though the woman reassures and encourages him, and leaves him the relatively safer inside position (i.e. not trapped on the rail), Shannon remains blocked. He does not feel quite comfortable in his own skin. What is expected of him here?

"You know what? We're going to pretend that you're all grown up!" The woman gets a saddle blanket and—very matter-of-factly—places it on the young stallion's back. She goes back and forth. Shannon waits. He concentrates: now something is happening to him! What is that? He listens behind him and pays attention to what the woman is doing. Then the saddle comes. Everything is done in a very relaxed way and without force, or pressure, the woman is not making a big deal of her actions. Instead, she always stays close to Shannon, praising and reinforcing him. He is never alone—she is there only for him, trying out a new game with him. The woman's attentiveness enfolds Shannon like a protective cocoon. There he can reflect on whether or not Kirsten's actions please him. Shannon does not have to play along in any way and he knows this. The least sign of unwillingness on his part would end the matter. This is a game Kirsten has devised for him. She is not calming him as they do this—why should she? He is not the least

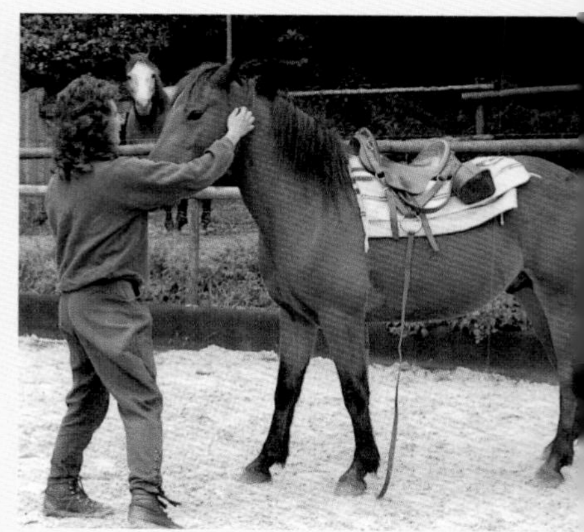

upset. She gives him a treat, strokes him, tightens the girth, and for the first time in his life, young Shannon experiences a blanket, saddle, girth, and stirrup irons on his body. No one has instructed him to stand still or be calm—and because of that, he is. This first saddling is an invitation that has been extended in complete harmony with Shannon's mood, and continually adapts to his changing state. Shannon can simply try out what Kirsten has conceived for him. Again the two of them run off together. At the trot, the stirrup irons bang against the saddle blanket. "What is that? Is someone up there?" Things seem a bit weird now to this young fellow. Shannon tenses slightly and because of that the blanket slips farther under the saddle as he moves. Kirsten is already there, she had noticed his uncertainty. And what does she do? She stands next to Shannon and pounds on the saddle! She increases the pounding. "Look, this is funny!" As I mentioned earlier in the book, this blind spot is where a horse cannot see what is going on (p. 19). Shannon cannot see well what Kirsten is doing, so he tries to feel. She is pounding on his back and

yet not on his back. How could that be? He backs up and thinks, "Odd sensation back there...not actually bad...just not something I'm used to."

Now he trots more confidently, that pounding doesn't matter. Then, in the last photo, the saddle is off and as at the very beginning the two of them are trotting another round together. Something has remained, but it is not the thing on the horse's back. Look at the young stallion's movement. It is different now.

The Inner Path

A horse's piaffe originates from an entirely different emotional state than a "dog trot" with sunken head. Nearly all the exercises that we human beings want to train our horses to do have a specific meaning in natural behavior. Each movement corresponds with a specific emotional state, and it is this emotional state that we can influence.

Feeling is movement, movement is feeling

If we change the horse's emotions to the good then the close connection between inner and outer suddenly begins to have a positive effect: good feelings create good movement and good movement creates good feelings. We know this reciprocal effect and use it ourselves to shake off a bad mood. Certain postures, if chosen freely, have a strong influence on consciousness. The energy of good movement usually stimulates and brightens gloomy moods. People are no different than animals. If I consciously decide to go dancing despite being depressed, dancing can change my mood because, like all movement, it has its own energy and this "statement," this external action, will be filled with that inner meaning that goes with it. However, that can only happen if my action is a conscious one and has not been forced on me. If I am forced to dance even though I do not feel able or willing, my inner state will deteriorate even further, my mood will get worse. So, to effect positive change, it is critical that actions be freely chosen and consciously taken.

Liberating the power

As soon as we consciously perceive the energy connected with a particular movement and allow it to work its effect on us, it can help and change us. Conscious movement can liberate inner powers. A timid posture and slack muscles will not allow a fighting spirit to arise. But, if you straighten and firm your back, if you stride consciously and powerfully so that you feel the ground's firm response with every step—all at once your eyes blaze and the feeling of strength is there!

Collecting the power

The connection between inner and outer energy can make lame or give wings, it can restrict or liberate, but it cannot be ignored or denied. The person who consciously perceives it can, by doing so, access and use, all his powers. This is why ancient Asian martial arts are also a mental discipline. This is why athletes pursue mental training, in order to concentrate all their power on the great feat. This is also why training horses on a mental basis is so enormously effective. With conscious movement, a horse opens himself to undreamed potential power, which otherwise would not, or would no longer be at his disposal. In this work with us, the horse finds his way to himself.

The Whole Horse

How does such work look? How does it begin? On the preceding pages, a horse-human encounter is depicted from start to finish. Shannon and Kirsten meet in the arena and the young stallion makes his first acquaintance with a saddle. In this session they start practically at the very beginning because in many respects it is a first time: Shannon does know Kirsten from grooming, feeding, and mucking, but other than that he does not know very much. He does not know that a person can be a playmate and a partner in learning, and he is not so constant an observer as Shane, who is the same age and is, as usual, observing us here (see his inquisitive face in the photo at the bottom of page 140). Shannon has not practiced or worked on any lessons. What should we call what he and Kirsten are doing? Play? Work? The person has a very special task and what should she be careful of, what must she take into consideration? Being with horses in this way demands great openness in every respect: a person must be constantly ready to accept and give sudden stimuli and aids, to build on situations that arise spontaneously, to take what has begun a step further and then let it go again. Creativity is required!

"Heaven is right where you are right now and that is the place to practice."
~Morihei Ueshiba, Founder of Aikido

But what is Kirsten actually doing? She runs with Shannon and then stops when she sees that he does not understand. She searches for another idea that might better suit him at this moment. She sees the saddle that by chance is still hanging there, and she improvises. Her awareness and caring create a safe atmosphere in which the young horse can confidently encounter all the newness. The relationship between horse and person is the decisive factor here. It allows spontaneous play to develop. As a "side effect" there is the matter of the saddle, but what is essential is the harmony, the dialog between the two of them. Their relationship creates their very own intimate world. In it, Shannon plays along without worry. He is totally open to Kirsten's ideas, and in the end he has gained something. Compare the photos of the young stallion before and after his encounter with the saddle. Do you see how differently he moves? The first pair of photos shows Shannon with slightly restricted movement and a slightly disoriented expression: the pulled-up right nostril, the twisted neck, the undirected ears. The indications are very subtle, but since we have become a bit more practiced in reading the horses' feelings, we can pick them up. Shannon's movements seem restrained, restricted, at the start. Look once more at the last photo. How does the young stallion feel now? A comparison makes clear that Shannon's whole carriage has changed. Suddenly his trot is rhythmic, powerful and balanced. There is a great difference between the last image and the first ones—and all in a quarter of an hour. How did this young horse get there so quickly? His feelings, his self-awareness and self-confidence changed! Do you remember when Kirsten rapped on the saddle and Shannon listened behind and felt what was happening rather than running away? At the beginning of their work together Shannon paid attention only to Kirsten, not to himself or to his own body. The experience with the saddle prompts him to direct his awareness inward, not only to the outside. After that, he moves more harmoniously and is at one with himself. Shannon feels his body more and so he leaves the encounter, not only with greater body awareness, but with greater self-confidence as well.

This way of working—sensitive, spontaneous, intimate

A horse transforms himself

Thinking with Horses

Customarily, a human being tries to get horses to follow his instructions. Horses are expected to understand him and do as he says. We will go the opposite way and try to follow the horses. We would like to understand them. What are horses saying to us? An encounter as harmonious as the one that was just shown is not possible when a person goes to the horse with a fixed agenda: "Today my horse will wear a saddle!" This kind of thinking is restrictive. The horse is not asked or invited—he is confronted with the person's determination. Such thinking destroys any sort of playful atmosphere, not because of the serious nature of the riding-related content of the exercise but because of the way the exercise comes to be, namely wholly without the horse's input. There is no togetherness in the process, no mutual ideas or thoughts that arise from an exchange between equals. There are only unilateral decisions on the person's part. But this kind of one-sided thinking has no place here.

The key to the work shown here is thinking with the horse. Conversations with horses cannot take shape in advance. The mental and spiritual connection cannot be forced. Every pre-planned idea dissolves in the spontaneous interplay of our mutual improvisation. Of course, it is highly important to be aware of what we are doing whenever we are with a horse. However, in our work, conscious awareness has a two-fold task. It must accompany all that we do together, and at the same time, it governs our own actions in every moment. This is not about a goal of some sort, like saddling, for example. It is about being awake in each moment to what is there, mustering all our sensitivity, and responding in suitable

Flexibility of the mind

A person's touch can be an invitation to feel one's own body more consciously. What you see here is not so much "praise" for Toppur (who in this photo is just finishing his "circle experience" from the last chapter) as a memory aid to help him recall that this area of the body was just now the most important part. I am letting what was just learned reverberate: "This is it! This is what it was about! You did that with your haunches." And the stallion looks and feels "back."

Aids should actually help the horse. What is most important is how my horse feels about an aid. Even a whip can be used in a positive, supportive way. But for that, it is necessary that my horse accepts this helpful tool and does not run away from it, that is, he listens "toward" the direction of the aid. Do you see Toppur's ear? The stallion is already trotting with rhythm and power not being produced by external means, but rather by the horse's increased awareness of his hindquarters, where the source of his power resides. Toppur does not duck away, yield, or fearfully tuck-in his rear end, rather he seems to spring even higher, toward the whip.

ways. Naturally, in order to rightly understand our horses we need a good deal of empathy, tact, and a wealth of ideas. But above all, we need the continually ongoing dialog with the horse: "What do you want? What can I do for you?" The fundamental condition for everything further is to not let this dialog break off.

In the work together, the person undertakes the assignment of finding the most suitable exercise for this particular horse in his current state from among the available choices. The inspiration for the right exercise usually comes very directly in the presence of the horse: Toppur turns a certain way, so we work on the circle. Shane fears "black holes" on the ground so we work with the tire. Hazel has her tendency to give up her space, give in, yield, so we practice travers. Passaro was hounded by his past so we practiced piaffe. Shannon avoids the connection with himself so he had a saddle placed on his back. Through working with human beings, horses begin to balance out their weak and wounded points and transform them into strengths.

Helping horses

Of Sense and "Nonsense" in the Exercises

The message a certain action sends a horse can vary widely depending on how we practice an exercise with him, in what connection and with what intention. When we do what we do with our horse's agreement, when we have his well-being in mind and this becomes clear to the horse, he will experience an exercise in a completely different way than if we did exactly the same thing for a purely arbitrary reason. Our action must have a purpose that is recognizably positive for the horse; it should not be performed just because the mood strikes us. Only in this way can the horse arrive at an "aha!" experience through performing a certain movement. Take, for example, walking backward—a movement that is non-habitual and seldom performed by a horse under natural circumstances. Forcing a horse to back up is a harsh correction, a disciplinary punishment that will quickly cause a fractious horse to give up and submit. Horses are reluctant to go backward because in doing so they go straight into the only area where they cannot see anything. Interestingly, when we work on this exercise with a horse, this completely understandable resistance disappears. Because our work is totally centered on the horse he can put aside his natural fear. And because of our very different way of working together, we discover in this exercise great possibility for positive change. A horse that is consciously stepping backward senses his own body, his own center, in an entirely new way. His awareness, usually "forward," now shifts back. Similar to a horse balanced in high collection, a horse consciously moving backward moves and carries his weight over the hind legs. He feels behind himself, in the direction of his hindquarters where the source of his power is.

Stepping backward into uncertainty

The right exercise is never a strait jacket. It is an offer. The horse can try the exercise and decide whether it suits him. Suitability becomes clear by the effect of performing the exercise; the horse will feel as good about himself as a person does when he wears a custom-tailored suit. Like a person wearing clothes that fit well, a horse performing the right exercise looks better and moves better. And like a person who is reluctant to remove his made-to-measure suit, the horse does not want to "take off" his "custom-tailored" exercise. An experienced trainer may find the most suitable exercise for a particular horse more quickly than the non-professional. But, in the end, it is the horse that fills the form of a movement with his inner power. He discovers the new exercise for himself—as Max did with Spanish walk. If trained by rote, an exercise remains an empty shell that leads a horse nowhere. When it is filled with meaning and experienced consciously, the right exercise can open a door for the horse into a new world. The exercises of the classical tradition carry both possibilities within them: forced submission and empowerment. They can

Straitjacket or custom-tailored suit?

be instruments of humiliation and pain, but they can also be the most potent remedies for healing the estranged body and the damaged psyche, and for giving the horse a whole new perspective of himself.

The Aids and Body Awareness

Aids to transformation

In order for a horse to further develop himself he must head in a specific direction, his work must have a goal. Suppleness and collection can become goals worthy of the horse's striving. Throughout, the horse can understand our intention—and he has the better sense of whether the work's direction is still correct because he directly experiences whatever change occurs. Nevertheless, he appreciates and seeks out the person's company and input on his path. As a rule, he will need us at least to create the environment in which this kind of work—playful and serious at the same time—is possible. The horse needs our help because it is not enough to practice and expect that all of a sudden piaffe will materialize. Exercises can convey very important feelings and sensations to the horse, but only if he understands the purpose of the exercise. Only a consciously performed movement has the desired potential for positive transformation. The critical aspect of a lesson is how the horse feels as he is doing it. Only if horses actually know what they are doing, can the benefit of the activity be comprehensive and long lasting. Whatever is done must be done in full consciousness, and this is where horses need our support.

Only when a horse no longer finds us—or our aids—in the least bit threatening can we work in the manner shown here: Toppur's path is bounded on the outside and I may not constrict him any further. But Toppur does not look as though he is frightened of moving along the fence into the more confined space. Even though the whip is pointed at him, he does not appear to feel confined or pressured. He trots confidently along and reaches with his outside hind leg as if in answer to the person's focused action. This is an empowered horse!

If a horse wants to progress with a certain exercise, perhaps for example, because he has a desire for collection, things can go with him the way they often go with a person: with the immediate goal before one's eyes, body awareness is diminished, perhaps even dangerously so. Surely you are familiar with the experience: you spill the coffee in your effort to get the butter, or you stretch to reach a book from the top shelf. You are almost there and suddenly, your stool tips over. In your eagerness and total focus on your goal, you have forgotten yourself. Your head and your awareness are already at your destination and are no longer connected to where your body is in that moment, so you can easily lose your balance. When you lose the connection to your own body because of your focus on the goal, you can easily over-face yourself and may even come to harm. On the path we travel with our horse, we will soon be more concerned with tempering his eagerness than with having to show him the goal. In this context, that entails reminding the horse to stay aware of his body and keep his balance. Once you have internalized that concept, the secret of giving the right aids will, without effort, be revealed to you. Even when a horse knows exactly what he wants, his human partner can greatly help him to maintain concentration so that in the process of transformation the horse does not lose the connection to himself.

Aids to consciousness

The "Right" Aids

A person who works with horses, who trains and rides them, knows many ways to get these animals to perform specific movements, measures that are supposed to "help" the individual horse understand and comply with the human's wishes. We speak of an "aid" but we could just as well use the words "command," "threat," or "punishment." Because logically structured systems are easier for human beings to deal with, riders learn this "aid-giving" as a set of rules, preferably with sketches that show them around the "dashboard" of this living sport machine. But to get a living being to function in such a predictable manner, a great deal of effort has to be invested to mechanize this creature and adapt him to the system. On this road to the goal of "animal automaton" occasional expressions of natural aliveness cannot be ruled out. When that occurs, disciplinary measures are used—sometimes harshly, sometimes more gently. Even then, the message that the individual horse receives will vary depending on the connection in which these measures are used and the intention with which they are employed. What is certain is that commands, intimidation, and punishment are not support for the horse and are neither desired nor welcome. As long as the person's actions are orders, threats, or warnings, the horse will pay more attention to these signals than to his own body, and his goal will be to protect himself from the anticipated pain. Instead of increasing his awareness of his body he will shut down his feelings because he wants to keep the threatened area safe. He tries to escape the effect of the horseman's action and therefore is fixated on it as though it were a red-hot glowing ember coming toward him. Conscious movement cannot develop this way.

Buttons, switches, and a users' manual?

Help, this is going to hurt!

Aids are useful to a horse only when they are not employed to enforce or reinforce the human being's superior power. We cannot arbitrarily classify the effect of aids on the horse as positive or negative according to general rules such as: weight aids are better; rein aids are worse; everything should be as subtle as possible. These external criteria do not necessarily or automatically apply to a sensitive, tactful dialog and a horse-friendly development program. On the contrary: it is possible for someone who has absolute power to speak very softly, or even merely raise his eyebrows—just a look will suffice—and his captive cringes in fear. So, what is important, what counts, is the intention behind the use of the aids and how the horse feels in the process. Do these aids serve the horse? In using

The inner criteria

Conscious Movement

Moving backward as an antidote to fleeing forward: the Connemara mare, Hazel is concentrating hard as she does it. It is easy to see how she listens within herself and finds her way into the steps. Walking backward is something horses rarely do on their own because a horse cannot see behind himself. In backing up he moves directly into the blind spot of his nearly 360 degree field of vision. But precisely because of this, moving backward is a very good exercise for developing body awareness. Of course, practiced this way the movement has nothing at all to do with submission or some kind of test of obedience. It has rather more to do with collection. The center of gravity is shifted toward the rear because the horse's attention is focused toward the rear. Hazel is not creeping backward nor bracing her forelegs, as is so often seen. She is not backing up because forward motion has been blocked or prohibited. Rather, she consciously chooses the direction in harmony with her human partner, who synchronizes her own steps to the mare's movement.

In the second photo you can see how Hazel takes her weight backward over the hind leg. First she moves her forelegs back, making her body shorter and rounder. Then she takes her weight backward and places her hind legs. In the last two photos she is beginning again with the front legs, licking as she does to release the mental tension resulting from her deep concentration. You can read it in her face and on the focused position of her ears. It demands a quiet, goal-oriented strength from a horse to listen within like this. My emphatic touch helps the mare maintain her concentration even through the steps of the movement, and steers her attention in the direction of the croup and hindquarters.

them, does the rider serve the horse, or is he just trying to enforce his own will? A horse does not care whether we label our efforts natural or unnatural, or whether they are visible or invisible to human onlookers. A horse simply wants to be free of fear and pain. That is what makes a difference to a horse.

The inner state of a horse is often not evident to an observer, particularly when the horse has had to learn that flight is useless and he has no recourse against the human being's power. Although he learns to do whatever is required, the horse always remains withdrawn in spirit. He reacts to negative stimuli that he wishes to avoid. This applies to all forms of manipulation in working with horses: even body language alone can be perceived as an "attack." Just because a horse is not physically touched by a person's movements does not mean that force is not being used. This is particularly the case in a confined space where the horse has no opportunity to retreat, as in a round pen, for example. After all, a situation does not become threatening only with the onset of physical contact. Threat arises long in advance of that, in the fear of the one being threatened "with the finger on the trigger." The person who pressures a horse against a wall or a fence or who drives him into a confined space is playing with the claustrophobia that is so much a part of the nature of these animals of the wide open spaces. Fear is, and will always be, the foundation of such work.

A frightened animal with the drive to flee

"The song of freedom cannot be played on the instrument of force."
~Stanislaw J. Lec

Find the Center

Centering: what does this word evoke for you? To center means to direct attention inward, toward one's own middle, to the center of power, the energetic center that is located about four to five centimeters under the navel. The Japanese call it "Hara," the "one point." It is the cornerstone for all types of meditation and is responsible for the building-up of physical strength. This is the body's center of gravity, and it is also an area that is in direct connection to our psychic energy. When we are successful in finding this point we set free great psychic energies that can influence our well-being in a spectacular fashion. Centering is a blending of spiritual and physical forms of energy that people in many types of sports are trying to produce through mental training. The knowledge of this center point as a source of power is ancient. In the Asian martial arts disciplines like judo, karate, kendo, and aikido, training on the mental/spiritual level is highly valued as an addition to the physical training. On the mental level, focus on one's own center is very important. Only then does the technical movement come. When the student has mastered the mental discipline he is totally focused, yet relaxed. He is at one with himself and his balance—and can then release all that gathered energy outward in an explosive concentrated form.

The one point

What does all this have to do with horses? Are we talking about throwing our horses to the ground with judo techniques? Of course not! Nevertheless, it makes sense to search for this point and involve ourselves with this process that will unlock our own powers. We need the art of centering. We need it for our horses, not in order to ride them but because we want them to use their whole potential. We want them to learn this art!

The centered horse

The art of centering is the art of collection.

The Nature of Collection

Collection: anyone who has been closely involved with horses and their use surely has views on this subject. Hardly anything else is so vehemently discussed by horsemen: what real collection is and what it is not, how it is achieved and how not, why collection is needed and why not. The various riding styles have very different views of collection. In general there is agreement that a horse that practices collection becomes more usable and useful—in other words, more pleasant to ride. In addition, he stays sound longer because riding is less harmful when the rider's added weight is carried by the muscular haunches. Now, there may be something to this, but you will not elicit a horse's enthusiasm for collection with the reason, "so that I can ride you longer and more easily." For a horse, this motivation is understandably not all that attractive. Why should he be interested in increasing his usefulness? Collection is strenuous and requires significantly more muscle power than what the horse needs in his everyday "energy-saving" mode. Who would volunteer to walk around with knees deeply bent? A horse particularly is unlikely to move in such an "uneconomical," wasteful manner of his own volition. That is why collection must be artificially developed, created by the rider—at least, that is what horsemen say. They maintain that genuine and free-willed collection is simply impossible. Why should a horse that is not being forced into it expend so much more energy of his own free will?

Collection as extravagance

The elements of collection have a thoroughly natural origin. We see them even in horses that live in freedom—in their tensing for a fight, in play, and particularly whenever a horse wants to impress others. We see the elements of collection in very specific situations in which a horse is not concerned about saving his strength but instead, with mobilizing all his power. He wants to test the competitor, measure his strength. Energy is overflowing then. Although in play horses seek to equalize the varying energy levels of the participants, the individual puts the overabundance of energy to use to show off, to impress, to declare, "I have more than enough."

Collection as luxury

However, in order for horses to behave in this way, they need a safe environment and a carefree atmosphere. A horse can only afford the luxury of using his energy extravagantly when he feels secure and when he is not being forced to move by external circumstances. A horse that naturally presents himself in a form that resembles classical collection feels pugnacious, in high spirits, proud, self-confident, and regal: master of the space, king of the steppes.

Enthusiasm and Emotion

What happens when a horse collects himself? We were able to see the principle in the previous chapter. When traveling on a curved line, our horse learned to move more collectedly, even if at first it was only to one side. When going around to the left, more was demanded of the left haunches, and going the other way, the right. In every corner and turn the horse practiced collection with the part of the body that was on the "inside." Now, he steps further under with both hind legs so that these come closer to the center of his body and no longer merely push, but also carry. With every step, the horse supports his weight more with his hind legs. He angles his haunches more sharply so that the whole croup is lowered and the movement impulse is forward-upward. The center of gravity of his body shifts further backward and the horse bends his haunches so that his forehand is freer and can become more elevated. In this way, he gains more mobility in all directions.

Steps to collection

With increasing collection the whole horse becomes more supple, and his responses become quicker. Although he now uses more muscle power, he is sparing and protecting his tendons, ligaments, and joints as the burden of every move, even the lateral ones, is absorbed, dissipated, and muted. His steps are powerful and light, the horse plays with his weight with the elegance of a dancer, and the elastic tension of his flexed haunches gives him the suppleness of a cat. Really, it must be a great feeling for my horse to move like that—and to feel so regal, assertive, high-spirited, and self-confident.

Self-awareness, self-carriage, and self-confidence: the secret of collected movement is pride and euphoria.

Collection as emotion

Before we ask for collection we must pose ourselves the questions: How does this horse feel? How does he feel in my presence? How good is he allowed to feel in my presence? Impressiveness requires a certain touch of arrogance, a sense of superiority, that "winning feeling." And play requires a feeling of freedom and light-heartedness—high spirits, in fact. Is my horse even allowed to feel so free, so proud, and so strong? Or is he expected to submit unconditionally to my dominance? For a horse to collect himself, his inner and outer powers must be harmonious and connected. If a person imposes a collected posture on him that is at odds with his inner disposition, this posture will fall off the horse like a badly glued-on shell. Free collection cannot be combined with subjugation or a feeling of submission. That is why, when collection is forced, the horse must be maneuvered into the desired posture over and over again. His inner feeling and outer form simply do not match. In such a case, is it not the person who wants to be impressive, to show himself off?

Standing fast and dancing

Collection is not for losers. If my horse avoids my presence and feels himself withdrawing, he will not even understand my efforts to get him to collect, except perhaps as an attempt to force him onto his "knees." Held in place and put under pressure, he may indeed bend his stifles and haunches, but clearly he will not be doing this out of a sense of his own power. A horse that is forced into defensiveness by the presence of a human being cannot afford to move with an extravagant expenditure of energy and strength. He does not know to what extremes he may be driven. Who knows how far he may have to flee? So, it is a contradiction of the most extreme kind to want to force a horse into collection. If he submits to the person's pressure he lacks the appropriate feelings of pride and high spirits. If he stands fast he remains in the old posture.

Consciousness in Movement

"I want you to feel yourself!"

How can we convey the feelings of the collected state to a horse? Is it even possible to influence a horse's inner condition from the outside? Can I do more than strengthen him in his individuality and pull myself back to give him more space? What can I do to change his consciousness, to make him feel better?

How do we make another human being aware of a very specific part of his body? If we are on intimate terms with him we do not think about it very long, "Oh, what have you got there?" We act spontaneously and lay a hand on that part of his body. Touching is the most readily available way to make him more conscious of the spot—a touch that is not demanding, but feeling, empathetic, giving the other person the gift of self-awareness. Empathetic touch—you do not need to use a complicated technique but just the "open" message, "I am here with you." And, "Try to feel here. Have you got it? Can you clearly sense this area?

Hand aids

How does that feel to you?" Hazel and I are having exactly this kind of conversation in the photo sequence on pages 150 and 151. I lay the palm of my hand on the muscles of Hazel's haunches and she brings her awareness toward me and begins to feel into her body because the path to me leads through it. From sensing her own body she develops the art of walking backward, hesitant at first but then with ever more intent.

The photos also show something else about this process: Hazel listens within herself and focuses on her own body. Consciously and in collection she tries the new movement. She begins with partial steps, starts each new step from within herself, and I accompany her. The steps we take together originate within the horse, from the sensation she experiences. The most important thing about what we do happens within the horse. In the third

On the Art of Finding the Right Spot

How does a person learn the "feel" for the right aids? Reno begins our first lesson in how to "sense" a horse by lying on the ground. This way he is less intimidating and can indicate the right spots calmly and with great patience. In the beginning we human beings must learn very concretely with our hands how what we do is received by the horse, as Reno demonstrates here with me. His pleased expression gives clear feedback.

In time, with such groundwork, a person develops a comprehensive feel and is able to sense the spot where a horse needs human aid, even when the horse is moving.

photo you can clearly see that it is not the person but the horse that begins the new movement. Hazel determines how we proceed. After all it is her body, her "feel."

Empathic, understanding touch can be an aid to direct the horse's awareness to his own body. But, in practice it is not always possible to lay a hand on a horse this way. This only works when we are standing still or walking slowly alongside one another. So, what do I do when my horse is moving more quickly? That is when a whip can be very useful—like an elongated finger, or a pointer. When the whip is used like that it bundles our concentration onto one point. All of my attention flows along the whip to the horse, to a specific part of his body, to which the horse's attention will then also flow. It goes without saying that my horse must have no feelings of fear or timidity about the whip—not even respect for it. If he did, his attention would be only on the whip so that he could keep himself safe from it and withdraw. But what I want is for my horse to increase his feeling of precisely the area to which I point, not withdraw awareness from it, or become tense or shut down. With the help of the whip I want to focus his attention, not upset him.

Whip aids

Keeping this in mind, have another look at the photos of my work with Toppur, particularly those in the previous chapter of him perfecting his circles. What is his attitude toward the whip? Does it change during the work? Along with the direct and indirect touching of the horse there are other very subtle aids that convey a message to him: namely, the quality of our own perception. When we look at a horse we share our presence with him. How we look at him plays a decisive role in how he perceives what we do. Here is where things become somewhat difficult because most people are not conscious of how they look at their horses, or how they see them. The horse on the other hand responds to the manner in which we look at him and what we perceive. That can become a problem when the relationship between horse and partner is a rather technical one. We human beings tend toward a way of seeing that can make a horse feel very insecure. The focused gaze that seeks visible weak points to attack, the predator's gaze, is sinister and threatening to him. He feels himself being appraised, watched. We human beings also do not like it when someone looks at us in this appraising way, even though we do not see ourselves as prey animals. Therefore, our attention toward the horse should be fundamentally passive, receptive, soft. In time we develop a sort of inner gaze that not only lets us see the surroundings but also sense them. Out of this rather diffused, holistic way of looking and perceiving, a precise focused look can become an important aid to a horse.

A way of "looking" that aids

In a previous chapter, Passaro found his way into passage from such a look (see page 131). You saw how Kirsten so empowered young Shannon with her comprehensive attention and empathy that at the end of the session he was more centered and could move more fluidly. And then there was my walk with Toppur at the very beginning of our journey through this book: just one look, an inner redirection of thought, influenced the stallion and led him back to himself. Thoughts and visualizations as aids?! We were with Shane as he tried to put his foot into the tire: apparently what we think is the most important way to influence a horse.

"I Do What You Think" or the Power of Our Mental Images

When I first met them the "thought exchange" between Passaro and Kirsten was already nearly perfect. At least, it seemed so. Passaro could read Kirsten's thoughts and communicated that way to her, when he wanted to. When he did, Kirsten sensed exactly what her horse was thinking and what was going on with him. Perhaps you are thinking to yourself, "Oh, I would like that with my horse, too." Kirsten, however, did not find this situation all that pleasant, and to explain why I will have to tell you a little bit about the two of them.

They met at a leasing barn where the dark chestnut was making his way on a trip to the slaughterhouse. All of the trainers had failed to break his resistance and make him docile. Kirsten, impressed by so much fighting spirit, paid for this obstinate character and bought the freedom of a purportedly treacherous animal with a terrible reputation, even though she herself was then living in totally uncertain circumstances. Her fascination with this rebellious horse was stronger than all powers of reason. Maybe Passaro knew, even then, how to communicate with her by thought. At any rate, when the two of them came to us Passaro was still, on the outside, a genuinely nasty fellow, one who attacked on all sides. But beneath that, a deep empathy connected him to Kirsten. Passaro was not simply "a horse" to Kirsten and Kirsten was not simply a human being to Passaro. He would bite at her and strike in her direction, but as soon as she planned to travel for a few days he would develop colic. That is how strongly her planned absences affected him. Their deep connection manifested itself rather negatively—he feared for her, she for him.

Of course Passaro had many quirks. Having once been kept in solitary confinement, one of them was that he became terribly agitated when we took a horse that happened to be a current favorite of his out of the herd. "He's going to crash through the fence!" Kirsten screamed in shock. Passaro had done that often enough in the past—just randomly jumped into something with great force—because he believed that someone wanted to keep him away from something or separate him. He could kick in all directions when he was convinced someone wanted to do something mean to him. Kirsten saw him pacing the fence line embittered, offended, hysterical, and she also saw where the fence was at its lowest. No sooner had she noticed that low spot than Passaro was over it, exactly where and as she had envisioned; he had picked up Kirsten's thought and acted on it.

"Not like that," I said to myself. There was no reason for him to behave like that. Passaro was not being left all alone—the rest of the herd was still there, and he was friends with those horses, too. We repeated the whole thing. I instructed Kirsten not to "encourage" her horse with her thoughts, but it was easy to see that this was too challenging for her in that moment. So, I let her take the other horse and sent her away. Passaro tried the same thing with me, the same wild decisiveness: "I'm going to jump...any second now."

"Sure, sure...," I thought, "and there will be a shock if you do. That's for sure."

Passaro hesitated. He was not prepared for this image. "These electric fences are really nasty...it is best to be careful, to keep a good distance from that fence." Passaro became uncertain. "What was that—an electric shock? Horrible! No one wants that...better stay away from that fence.... Actually, it is pretty silly to be pacing back and forth.... The others are standing in that luscious grass over there filling their bellies...."

Again, I did nothing but stand there, very relaxed, actively creating a mental image of the grazing horses. Passaro thought it over. He became very quiet and behaved exactly as I had envisioned it.

Kirsten had unconsciously given him the mental support to jump. I now used the same channel to give Passaro an image of sensible behavior. By the way I constructed my mental images I gave him a suggestion for a different way to act. Perhaps we can imagine this as an idea that suddenly came to Passaro from outside himself, an inspiration that he "found" the way a person suddenly finds the right word. The idea struck him as "not such bad one" and in the end he was totally pleased with himself.

The mental aid is based on the horse's ability to intuitively sense the feelings and intentions of other living beings, whether dangerous or friendly. This ability is well known to many horse people: for example, the horse that does not allow himself to be caught because the vet is due to arrive soon. Then there is the horse that senses his rider's fear of

Thought transfer

the obstacle and refuses to jump, or the horse that anticipates the commands of his rider. Usually such behavior strikes us as negative, but the ability of a horse to sense the feelings of another is always there. Whether or not we acknowledge it, horses do connect with us. Perhaps their forebears had to develop a sense of the danger posed by human beings—for similar reasons as zebras with lions. At any rate, not all horses are as masterful at this as Passaro, and above all, not all of them can use this ability so intentionally to their own advantage. In hindsight, it is not surprising that this rather slight, fragile Arabian could successfully resist even the toughest men: he looked for his opponent's weakest point simply by examining him, and at the right time, reacted resolutely and with astounding success.

Exactly how horses do this is an interesting question, and perhaps one day there will be a scientific explanation. But, at the moment, it is of much more interest to consider how we can utilize this ability in our work. The horse, and above all, the human being can both learn to use this special talent of the horse for more positive and intimate understanding of one another. It is not only with horses like Passaro that work with mental images is very successful. Mental images are available all the time. There is a mental/spiritual channel that connects human and horse. It is always there but using it consciously and in a positive way is not always easy.

Thought discipline

To do that, we need a certain kind of mental discipline. We must learn to direct our thoughts more consciously. When I tell myself not to think of chocolate, that is when that undesired image appears in my mind. Then I think of chocolate up in the cupboard, see the packaging in my mind's eye, hear the crinkling of the paper, taste the flavor on my tongue...even though I do not want to, in fact, just because I do not want to. So that does not happen, I must proactively think of other things—a sweet juicy orange, a steaming cup of coffee, or a vacation day at the beach with the water, the warm sun, the sense of expansiveness. When I am with my horse I should also think about good alternatives so that he does not fixate on undesirable thoughts. Chocolate is a harmless image but what happens if I paint myself a lively picture of my horse bolting, bucking, or shying? He might do exactly what I fear simply because no other clear image occurs to either him or me. Develop positive images for your horse!

Freedom of thought

To avoid any misunderstanding, I want to make it clear that the mental connection to a horse is absolutely not an instrument of force or control! It defies any attempt at dominance. A horse cannot be manipulated or hypnotized by the power of thought, steered by a type of mental remote control (fascinating as this idea might be to some, given the insane conceit of our times). A horse will break the connection very quickly when a person behaves inappropriately or tries to press his advantage to the horse's detriment. "No thank you!" And that would be the end of that. Perhaps that is exactly why our ability to visualize can be such a powerful aid—it is free of any kind of force. However, coupled with some sort of forceful measure, a mental image will have a very massive effect, but sheer mental power alone will not enable anyone to exercise force. Thoughts are free. We can, with our thoughts, show a horse certain behavior, but he is in no way bound to behave as we visualize, and will decide for himself whether or not to act on our images. He does not have to use my idea. Even if my thoughts are the impetus, my horse acts of his own volition. This quality is what makes mental support so ideally suited to a horse in collection.

Symbols of Collection

Among human beings where the principle of human dominance reigns supreme, one rarely finds the emotional base required for a horse to move in collection. This emotional

The Centered Horse

Max, who today is such an impressive athlete, shows us once again what transformation means. Through conscious schooling of his body he has made a totally different horse of himself. The time elapsed between the photos on the left and those on the right, is two years. Interestingly, we see him here not only in the same gait, but also in the same attitude and mood, namely, at play. In those two years Max so fundamentally changed his habitual carriage that he seems much more compact and powerful. The powerful uphill canter, the collected trot in self-carriage, but most fascinating is his aura, the power he radiates: regal, dignified, collected, at peace with himself. Max has found his inner strength, the source of collected power.

state, the foundation for collection, is one in which consciousness of power and invincibility finds its physical expression. The feeling, "I can do anything," has grown out of the certainty that "I do not have to do anything I do not want to do." With this fundamental conviction a horse can see his way clear to "squandering" his energy on extravagant collected movements. Schools of riding that traditionally placed great value on a horse's impressive carriage were therefore careful not to break the spirits of their young horses. It had to be like that because they wanted to develop their horses' ability to collect. "We shall take care not to vex the horse, or cause it to abandon its grace and sweetness in disgust," said French horseman Antoine Pluvinel to his King in the seventeenth century, "for this is like the fragrance of blossoms, which never again returns once it has vanished." This realization, which he put so poetically into words, has been nearly forgotten by the horsemen of our time. Quick and practical methods of "breaking in" are preferred, and they are intended to drive out the horse's every resistance from the very start. Their stated purpose is to make the horse the most smoothly functioning piece of sport or leisure equipment possible. A horse's individuality is rather bothersome from this perspective. With these methods a rider may, perhaps, have a comfortably serviceable animal, but not one who will bloom and bear fruit as Pluvinel meant. The personality of a horse must be preserved and allowed to develop in order for his path to genuine collection to be possible.

The spirit of a king...

Centering is uniting inner and outer powers. A horse that collects himself concentrates his energy around his body's center of gravity, which has moved a bit further toward the rear and lies a bit lower than usual. He "sits down" as he seeks his own center point. In all cultures there are spiritual practices intended to help human beings find their center. But, the center of inner and outer balance is not a fixed, static point. A person can lose his center and find it again like a top that spins, tips, and rights itself again as long as it keeps moving. Centering is coming back to oneself, to the center of the cyclone, again and again. Perhaps you have seen a horse collected like this: he is round, concentrated, a ball of energy. The strength of the hindquarters, formerly employed only to push the horse forward, is now under his center of gravity. The angles of his joints have become tighter; they have taken on weight and are carrying it; they are like coiled springs, prepared to shoot off at any time. It is not external pressure or force that flexes the haunches of a collected horse. In full consciousness of his own power he brings himself into this state of high tension. He gathers his energy into one point to increase his elasticity, like a tiger before he pounces.

The power of a tiger...

A proud and self-confident attitude cannot be produced with force. Forceful measures only cause the seed of sovereignty within every horse to be lost forever. True collection is an inner bearing that develops slowly at first; it is a ripening process. A good education can support and further this because it is absolutely possible to coax a trusting, befriended horse into collection. I can create a playful, relaxed, euphoric atmosphere and encourage him to experiment with his center of gravity. I can reinforce his self-confidence. At some point my horse will begin to collect himself when he is with me, because collection will be an appropriate expression of how he feels. And all at once he will feel more agile and supple, loaded with energy—just as Joy did in the last chapter when she discovers how quickly she suddenly can turn. Or like Passaro, who meanwhile has a preference for magnificently celebrating himself by moving in collection. Or like Toppur who, at the beginning of this chapter, proudly expresses his Icelandic nobility with an elevated canter. Or like Mighty Max, who, given wings by his mental power, overcomes his physical limitations. Or like Reno, who strives for the capriole in order to bring it all to the right point. Oh, and then we still have El Paso, who by collecting himself, succeeds in winning over the lady he loves...

...and the song of love

When the Powers Flow Together

The goal of our work is a strong horse, strong in every sense. My horse walks this path and I accompany him. I make sure he has the space, the peaceful environment, and a structure for the work—but I do not in any way disturb him with constant correction or distract him with an attitude of "I know better!" Working with a horse like this means joining him in the search for the center, the point of power, the heart of all activity. It means showing him various possible ways to collect himself and letting him choose. It means working with him to find exercises that he sees as genuine aids because they make it easier to do what he wants to do: feel good! If what we do is correct, we will have to make an effort to control our horse's enthusiasm for the work—after all, what could be more fascinating than discovering one's own power?

Connected with the energy

Work with a horse will change completely when he no longer avoids our suggestions but, instead, greets the aids. At the beginning of this chapter Toppur, our Icelandic guide, shows himself off in a highly collected canter in self-carriage (page 134). Such strides demand a very focused use of his entire body, and in the free space of the arena Toppur takes responsibility for balancing himself—only my voice assists him in this effort. A horse that has been schooled on a mental level responds to the concentration of his human partner in a totally new way. He no longer protects or pulls away the body part in question ("Help! I know I will get hurt, I have to watch out, I have to get away!") Rather, he too focuses his awareness there. It is no longer threatening when the person concentrates. The horse does not feel he has to flee to safety just because the person takes "aim"—with a whip, for example, or with his mental focus. On the contrary, the horse responds to his human partner likewise and focuses his awareness in the same area. This directed awareness unlocks the horse's enormous potential power. He learns to develop himself, to school his body, and to consciously collect himself.

The power of concentration

A horse that follows commands out of obedience to the person or from fear of "correction"—even when these are not evident at the moment—will never be able to find a deeper self-improving reason for them on his own. He will never truly derive benefit from the exercises he performs because he never experiments with and explores these movement patterns for himself. He does not further develop these patterns independently, he is not really aware of what he is doing. What is achieved by this kind of "following orders" is actually the opposite of conscious movement. It is subjugation by an external element, namely, the rider.

Because it is in his nature to strive for harmonious relationships a horse will, as a rule, do what we demand of him insofar as he possibly can. But when exercises are done in that spirit, their deeper sense and purpose will always remain incomprehensible to the horse. Collection as obedience remains empty form. A broken horse forever remains a subordinate riding animal and, under human domination, will never find his true power. He will never become that creature of our wildest dreams, a marvelous, powerful, exuberantly happy presence, bubbling over with the joy of living.

The fire from within

The Magic of the Emotions

Bernd, our photographer, caught an interesting episode that took place near the riding arena: little pinto El Paso had just finished working in the arena with us, and had learned something important about the concept of collection. He had performed one or two particularly beautiful movements that conveyed the feel of passage to him. Swelled with pride he leaves the arena fully aware of his power and ability.

Then something unusual happens! El Paso goes to a manure pile, sniffs, leaves his mark—his energy radiance is very different than usual. Atila, the regal lead horse and guardian of the mares, is dazzled by the radically transformed little guy and, bewildered, clears out of his way. It is as though El Paso suddenly had special powers. He feels like Superman, and looks it. Because of El Paso's impressive carriage the nearly 20 cm difference in height between the two horses is barely noticeable anymore.

This incident is particularly noteworthy because these two geldings have known each other for quite some time, and El Paso, like a typical bottom-of-the-pecking-order horse had never even thought of disturbing the "gentlemen" at the "executive level." And there was someone else impressed by the "new" El Paso, though there are not pictures to show it. Hazel was interested in the lively pinto and had tried several times to flirt with him. Atila had always strictly forbidden it. Until today, El Paso had not dared even to look in Hazel's direction. But moments after these photos were taken, Hazel joined her victorious knight in a brief, intense love affair. She disappeared out of sight with her new lover and basked in his unbounded admiration.

VFL
VFL

“We are not the only creatures in the world whose feelings matter.”

~Jane Goodall

Strong Horses—Strong Friends

Horses among Themselves

Horses do not ride one another. No horse shuts another in a stall or ties him up. Horses do not build fences and they know no limits such as borders and property lines.

Even though these animals do not use one another, they choose to live in groups. They did this even in their original home on the endless steppes. What binds them together is neither fear nor force, nor is it the prospect of an organized hunt such as a pack of wolves might undertake. Although the horses' sources of sustenance are rather spread out over a large area, they like to be near one another. They like each other, although not indiscriminately—they definitely have their preferences. Horses develop close friendships. What governs the togetherness of the herd is the bond of affection that is continually maintained and strengthened by each individual animal's friendly attentiveness.

The bonds of friendship

War and Peace

It is odd that, on the one hand, we use horses for therapeutic purposes because they are such generous creatures and so empathetic to the weaknesses of ill people and children, and on the other hand, we maintain that without strict discipline and the principle of the human being as the permanent leader they would be a threat to the human being. The constant repetition of such theories says far more about us than about the nature of horses.

Who is really threatening whom here? A horse makes every effort not to step on the fallen rider who had just been mercilessly abusing him. Even in a clear fight situation horses, as a rule, avoid the counter-attack if they can. If they do offer resistance it is usually out of fear because they can see no other way out. Horses do not gain anything from exploiting weaknesses or making prey of other creatures or injuring them. Even a fighting bull must first be goaded to attack. Apparently human beings are very inclined to attribute behavior to horses that is rather more descriptive of themselves—or, if you prefer, a hungry predator.

Is the horse a danger to the human?

I once knew a stallion that was difficult and aggressive and spent the better part of his day running back and forth in a dark box. His caretakers could barely manage him, but there was one trick that could, without fail, quiet this restless horse. When enough bedding straw was put into the box so it came up to his hocks, he would immediately move only in slow motion. The solution to the puzzle was a rabbit that lived in the stable. It hopped around freely and often visited the stallion's box in order to eat some of his grain. When the straw was piled high the stallion could not see the rabbit and out of fear of inadvertently stepping on him he hardly dared take a step anymore. This horse was frustrated and enraged at the general circumstances of his life yet he, on his own, controlled his agitation—all for the sake of a small thieving rabbit.

We human beings begin robbing horses of the awareness of their own strength when they are still at a tender age. We accustom them to their powerlessness and our arbitrariness. Foals are not as strong as full grown horses and make fewer difficulties when we forcefully subjugate them. We hold them fast, immobilizing their small bodies by bending their sensitive docks upward, the first halter is clapped on the head and then the foal is dragged here and there at the end of a rope. No one gives much thought to how the foal feels about this. And what does the "horse-child" learn from this experience? Is it that raw force is the language of human beings and that there is no alternative for him but to

Dance of joy: a horse playing freely and freely collecting himself. On the same level as the human being he discovers his powers. He feels strong and irresistible. In a dialog with his two-legged partner and friend this horse gives expression to his carefree feeling. Light as a dancer he displaces his weight to his hind legs and embodies the reason he was created: movement, the joy of living, the lightness of being.

The Big Show

What is going on here? Kirsten and Max are playing a "war game" with one another. With the courage of a lion Mighty Max defends his territory—the riding arena—against the "evil whip-wielder" so brazenly taunting him! Horses that were once shy have an especially great sense for such games. They love to act "as if" and enjoy their rediscovered strength. Max is in high spirits. Catlike, he flies over the sand completely in tune with his role as king of the arena.

Only a deep, safe, mutually trusting relationship permits games with pseudo-aggressive elements, just as teasing and a certain kind of joking are possible only between people who are very devoted to one another. Between strangers, or in situations without a prior understanding and friendship, such games are pure provocation that can result in irritation or even genuine aggression. But, between good friends, they are a sign of high spirits, the best possible disposition.

Or, is the human a danger to the horse?

acquiesce to the incomprehensible? Maybe he gives up, becomes spooky, is frightened by nearly every gesture. At any rate, a young horse treated this way cannot understand what we want of him, and at some point he will stop trying to understand. But, there is another way to communicate, even with a foal. Instead of simply bullying and intimidating a young horse, we can offer him real aids, explanations, affection. Even though we are still more powerful than he is, we can consider his feelings and treat him lovingly and with respect. Is that not how we would like to be treated by him in the future?

The Resonance of Emotions

Reciprocal effects

These days, the moment a horse encounters us he has already lost a great many of his opportunities for a free existence. Whether for a person or a horse, powerlessness and close confinement are among the most deeply discouraging, depressing situations imaginable, and they are connected with one another. An individual who feels powerless will hardly be able to enjoy the freedom of greater space, and one who feels empowered will not so easily feel pressured, and therefore will deal better with confinement. In our work, we have reinforced the horse in safeguarding his position and expressing his feelings. Instead of "naming the tune" and using our whip as a metronome to superimpose our own "beat," we have searched for the music the horse senses within himself. That way, we achieve a shared tune, because each of us listens to the melody of the other. Horse and

"I am strong! I can do even more!" Getting the feel of their own bodies makes even insecure horses "conqueror" types. We have made the horse the main focus of our thoughts and actions instead of simply demanding that he comply with our demands and desires. The mare, Joy, having become empowered by working this way, does not want her newly rediscovered strength taken away so quickly. As I begin to dismount, she throws a nearly indignant glance my way, as if to say: "What?! You want to quit already?" She clearly does not feel like a subordinate creature at the end of our riding session—she is the carrying member of our relationship! She does not want to quit yet—we both benefit from our arrangement.

The victorious horse

partner "jam" with one another, alternating or in unison develop new possibilities, new variations on their theme, and like voices of two unique singers blend into the overriding unity of their duet. Their resonance carries them both onward, they cannot resist its power, and together they create a completely new experience of movement—a synergistic experience that strengthens both of them.

A self-aware, independent, empowered horse moves in majestic carriage and with elevated paces. His bearing is powerful but nevertheless light, springy, and elastic. He radiates a joy in being alive and his enthusiasm is catching. His collection never results from dominance or hierarchy. It comes from the feeling of being free and in full possession of his own power. Only a self-aware, empowered horse is able to carry himself in this way. Collection is the foundation for doing battle and for behavior intended to impress. It is how a horse gathers his power so as to be able to safeguard his rights in the blink of an eye. It is this "fighting spirit" that creates the aura of a collected horse. This connection between inner and external power is very real to horses, as El Paso showed us so indisputably in the previous chapter. When a horse begins to learn genuine collection he is learning nothing other than the equine version of martial art.

"As the housewife who has scrubbed the floor sees to it that the door is shut so that the dog cannot come in and undo all her work with his muddy paws, so European philosophical thinkers have guarded against any animals tramping on their systems of ethics."
~Albert Schweitzer "Philosophy of Civilization"

Us and Them

Words fail me...

When we first begin to seek an understanding with a horse, the language barrier seems insurmountable. But as soon as we expand our powers of imagination and move beyond our limitations, we become able to observe things that we could not see before. The world of feelings is present everywhere. In it, human beings and horses can communicate directly and immediately with one another. Will we ever know for certain what horses feel? No, but that is something I cannot know about you either, despite our common language. In the course of our lives we human beings spend a great deal of time confronting our own feelings and those of our fellow humans. Speech as a tool of creating understanding does not solve the problem. Ultimately we can only draw conclusions based on the behavior of our counterpart. But what exactly is he feeling? What does he mean when he says "I love you"? What does she mean when she says, "I love you"? Not the same thing, I think. Your feelings are not mine, even if we both use the same words to describe them. When we venture with our horses into the territory of our common feelings, we violate the carefully guarded boundaries of an old prejudice that says only he who can express himself audibly, with words, is entitled to an inner life worthy of consideration. But even those who have no words or to whom speech comes less easily—"strong silent types," babies, the sick, the elderly, or animals with their different language—have feelings and the ability to think.

Actually, the knowledge of the emotional receptiveness of horses for what human beings communicate is not new. It was so obvious that it found its way into common German expressions like "coaxing someone as you would a sick horse." This animal apparently understands a person who speaks to him with a sense of urgency.

A human being has the power to reach a horse emotionally—for good as well as for evil. The roots of the horse's receptiveness probably lie less in humankind's God-given greatness than in our common history: the horse a prey animal and man his most dangerous hunter. So effective a hunter was man that today there are no more true wild horses. Is it surprising that the survivors, today's horses, understand our body language and seem to know our intentions?

Mastery of a horse is easy to obtain: his inborn timidity opens up the path to his psyche. The horse will submit to the person who behaves like a predator. The horse will even follow such a person if all possibility of escape has been blocked off and only this option remains. Survival in captivity depends on following and obeying the captor. Winning a horse's friendship, however, is an entirely different goal than forcing his submission, and leads us down completely different paths. I cannot change the fact that I am a human being and my counterpart is a horse. But, instead of using my power and privileged position against the horse, I can put them at his disposal to help him. I can show him that I am a congenial companion, and I can minimize my threat to him by giving him power over me and letting myself be influenced by him. That does not mean sitting there doing nothing or leaving everything to the horse—although even such behavior can be appropriate on occasion. Instead, we try to carry on a two-way conversation and get to know one another: it is a dialog by which we all surpass ourselves, we grow beyond our limitations. Without this mutual exchange, what we show in this book is unimaginable. An overriding unity has grown step-by-step—one that lets us hear the music of the other and makes possible intimate games like the one between Kirsten and Max. A horse must feel not only free but also wanted, loved, and irresistible in order to accept the playful challenge of a human being as a friendly one, and respond with joy.

Beyond dominance

Horse World and Human World

Moving together on the same level and sharing feelings—this primal form of communication was in place between Toppur and me at the very beginning of our walk together. Being on one wavelength creates receptiveness for each other's feelings. Every one of us can listen from within ourselves to understand, without need of fancy words, what the other means. That is how we avoid misunderstanding. For example, if I unintentionally make a hasty movement with the whip, my horse will not be startled by it because he is not reacting solely to external actions but to my mood and feelings. And I react to his: he will no longer take me completely by surprise with his behavior when we are riding out because I now sense in advance what he would like to do and can adapt myself accordingly. We share each other's worlds and know each other well. This mutual receptiveness makes for sensible, reasonable horses. They trust their partner's concern for them. And if one is training horses, isn't it brilliant to be able to reinforce them as soon as they even think of doing the desired thing?!

From me to you, from you to me

As I was still reflecting on this subject of mutual receptiveness, Toppur suddenly appeared in my thoughts and made an incident that occurred here in the spring come alive again in my mind. Everything was erupting in the warmth—including the horses' hormone levels. "Oh, no! The stallions are loose!" I manage to catch up with one of them, Shane, not yet old enough to understand what the excitement is about, near the house. But Toppur, accompanied by Max, is thundering determinedly across the field in the direction of the mares.

It is May. The boys, fired by the power of sexual attraction, have already run hundreds of meters through hip high grass. It is a catastrophe in the making. Or, is it? I shout, "Get away from the fence you silly mares!" Oh dear, one of them seems to be in season. Images shoot through my head—the whole herd, incited by the stallions, running loose through the village in a wild panic...

The unbound stallion

Now I am in the field—the fencing is still intact but the horses are running alongside it. The stallion is beside himself with lust, the mares are squealing. I cannot get them to stop—only their rules apply now.

I am exhausted. My lungs ache, the landscape is spinning before my eyes, I can barely get enough air to speak: "Toppur! Toppur, please, please. Toppur!" My knees are shaking, I am near collapse. With my last bit of energy I try to focus on the horse, there is no other

On the Art of Collecting Oneself

Here Reno is concentrating so intently that he does not even glance toward the camera as he would typically do. Nearly all of his attention is required for what he is doing. To the collected horse everything external becomes insignificant. The connection with the person takes on another dimension. The horse collects around himself, searches for his own middle, the center of energy, the still point of movement.

By running beside and then ahead of Reno, Kirsten is trying to draw him out of his balled-up concentration so that he does not overwhelm himself with his uncompromisingly sought tension and flexion. The person sets the framework, creates the atmosphere, and makes his ideas available—the horse begins to dance with his own carrying power, celebrating himself.

alternative. I try to reach him with my thoughts. I speak only to him saying his name over and over, imploring: "Toppur!" And...he listens to what I am saying. "Please, Toppur, don't do it. I can't run anymore. I'm afraid for all of you." He lowers his head and looks at me, hesitating. He is completely still. I go to him and slowly fasten rope and halter. Then I lead him back, right past the mares. My heart is full to overflowing. Toppur neighs, rears, and puts on a show, so that all the mares can admire him as he makes his exit.

The Effect of the Neutral Zone

On our journey through this book we have let ourselves be guided by our exchanges with our horse and always sought overriding unity in our interactions. We have given our horse space, felt the kinship between us in wild and gentle games, and so were able to experience a nearly healed world, one that transcends the conflict of everyday reality. Together we created a new reality, our own "playroom," a shared space for experimentation, a very special place between the worlds.

The wisdom of the body

Here problems resolve as if on their own because of the positive healing effect our euphoric movement has on body and spirit. Not only have back and leg problems dissolved into thin air, but with his transformed presence, the horse even uses his feet in a new way, sparing them irregular and unnecessary wear and tear. This was particularly noticeable in Passaro who used to wear his hooves very unevenly and now goes straight. What is most impressive, however, is how lively and energetic horses become once they connect with their own ability to move. Their euphoria is like an awakening. Their enthusiasm becomes intoxicating, ecstatic. A horse estranged from himself may seem lazy and dull, but what he is really lacking is knowledge of his own power.

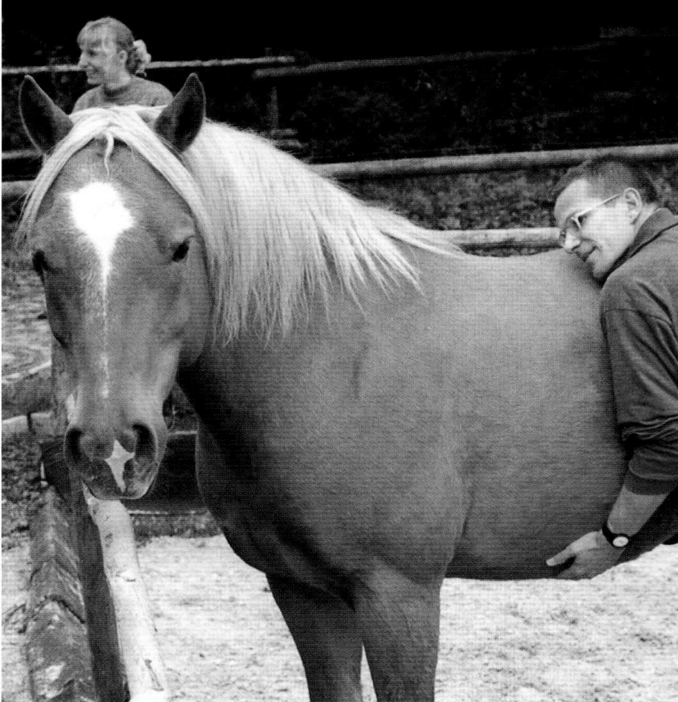

Even when playing wild games, empowered horses immediately sense when things become too much for their playmate and they restrain themselves. Periods of carefree play alternate with quiet, intimate moments. The horses adapt themselves to the feelings of the human partner and behave accordingly. In the photo at the left it is lovely to see Kim's pronounced play expression while he nevertheless "listens within" to preserve the contact with his own body. Body-awareness, self-awareness and collection belong together. Note the easy deep bend of the haunches in both horse and human.

Our horse enters the arena like a conquering hero. His step is elastic, springy. He commands the stage. He plays the role of his life: here his world is in order again, here things are seen in their proper light, put in their proper place...because here the horse is master of himself, a king in his realm. He feels strong, proud and free. The arena belongs to the horse. It is his stage, the place where he plays the leading role. He is enthralled with his might, commanding, sure of himself. His muscles conform to this image—all at once his bearing becomes as magnificent as he feels. Impressive! And then he moves that way too—grandly, extravagantly. Piaffe, pirouette, levade, capriole—those are movements of the greatest power, yet they are performed virtually on the spot. Collection is a horse asserting himself, claiming his rights and his space. He wants to stay where he is. It is the total opposite of running away. The horse feels safe, he does not fear whips, riders, harsh words; rather, he stays cool and calm, relaxed. He does not flee at the crack of the whip. Instead, he regally asks, "Pardon me?" Yes, the old-time horse trainers will say this horse is disobedient and cheeky, but they do not notice the sparkle in his eye. And as they indignantly turn away, they completely miss the horse's movement, more wonderful than it has ever been, in response to his human friend's pleased laughter.

The lazy horse

"In order to allow something to become a reality, we must first think it."
~Albert Einstein

The Friendship of Horses

Opening up to the horse and his feelings also means becoming more open with ourselves. Why do I do what I do? What is it that I want to achieve by this? When we discussed body language we came up with this: in this path to the horse there is no substitute for honesty and sincerity. Lack of integrity not only sends the horse a confusing message, it also prevents trust from growing within myself. To achieve inner harmony, I need to be clear about my feelings and be in accord with them. This honesty about and with myself strengthens the trust between me and my horse, as well as my willingness to show him even those feelings I do not like—the fearful ones that we so seldom acknowledge. Yes, the fears! These feelings, which are omitted as far as is practicable from a relationship with horses based on subjugation, here become an important element of our mutual friendship. There is no need for me to gloss over my weaknesses. Rather, I show them to my horse very clearly. I want him to know how strong he is. I will be traveling a long road with this horse, entering into an intimate relationship with him, even allowing myself to be carried by him. From this perspective, it is quite dangerous when a horse in close interaction with me has an inaccurate sense of his physical strength, because then he will not know how easily injured and fragile I am and he might interact with me as he would with a much more robust horse friend. He should know that I am not a "superhorse." In all our interactions—even in our playing together—it is important that my horse does not see me as another horse, but rather understands me and our relationship as something unique and special. He should understand that I do not behave as horses do because, after all, I am not a horse. I am different. I am a human being.

A special connection

For a new relationship paradigm to develop between man and horse, completely different thinking is required. The bond of friendship is a foundation that must be carefully built and maintained. As the human being I must be the one to do the work of persuasion since I am the one courting my horse, seeking his friendship. My horse will respond to what I bring to him, and if we are truly close to one another I will never feel the need to deliberately test our connection. In an emergency, my horse will be as open to my feelings as I am to his. Toppur did not exercise his advantage over me. Why did he not use the opportunity he had? I had no way of controlling the situation and all the horses knew this. They demonstrated this when they ignored me and ran to another section of the fence.

Even when a horse is still small and we are stronger than he is, we should not subject him to force in our interactions. A youngster is not yet as stable in mind and body as a mature horse, but he would like to be just as respected and lovingly treated. That way he will not need to be frightened by new challenges but can approach them bravely and with composure.

Little Shane is alone in the arena. The two photos show him before and after his first encounter with a rope and being led.

A special situation

Had I been a horse, even a higher ranking one, and had stood in Toppur's way, he would have fought me for the mares that were almost his. He would have fought with anyone in such an exciting situation, even with a horse with whom he was close friends. Why did Toppur listen to me when I had reached the "end of my rope," when I was at my wits' end?

I have never exploited this horse's weaknesses to my advantage. Rather, I have reinforced and strengthened him however I could. Perhaps Toppur was responding to that, and did not use his strength against me in a countermove just as I had never used mine against him. There is an old law about energy that states that every connection always works both ways. Perhaps Toppur experienced what some of us do, when after a time, we are so directly in tune with our horse's feelings that it is nearly impossible to disregard them, so emotionally permeable have we become. It seems that horses, too, cannot tear themselves away from this two-way connection.

Being emotionally transparent: it works both ways

The Transformed Horse

Compassion and empathy: if we want to work with a horse in this way we are not his master. Rather, the horse is master of himself. Of course, this requires a sovereign, independent horse, a horse that has learned to follow his own path, who knows and trusts his own power, and to whom—precisely because of that—I can entrust myself because he knows what he is doing. Everyday dangerous situations arise when horses do not know their own strength. Kim, our Haflinger, was such a case. At one time, it took great effort just for him to put one foot in front of another because inwardly he held himself in such high tension. His power would suddenly explode through him and he would shoot off like a stray bullet until he blindly stumbled down a slope somewhere. Kim had no idea that people might be afraid of him; he saw himself as clumsy and stupid and every two-legged creature seemed vastly superior to him.

Kirsten, who experienced this period with him, just could not manage to forget her feelings from that time. Even though she knew how much Kim had changed since then,

In the life of a horse there are always things that he fears, that he does not trust himself to do, or that he does not understand. In these situations the person can assume the role of helpful advisor; he can offer his support and encourage the horse. When we have assured the horse that we will stay with him, he no longer needs to shy away, even from difficult tasks that would make him feel over-faced if he were on his own. Here is the young stallion, Shane, a few minutes before his encounter with the tire—the "moving" hole in the ground (see page 95).

she could not trust herself to accept his challenge to play the way all the other people did without a second thought. In our chapter on play we saw Kim with Hans-Peter and with Waltraud, but Kirsten always declined Kim's invitation and preferred to look on. One day, Kim was again engaged in wild play with Hans-Peter, explosively galloping hot on the man's heels when Hans-Peter suddenly fell down. In a fraction of second Kim was standing stock still, as though rooted to the spot. We were shocked, believing for a moment that it had been Kim who had caused Hans-Peter's fall. Kim, on the other hand, looked surprised at the sight of Hans-Peter lying at his feet and seemed to say, "Hey there, that is an unusual way to test my reaction time!" Hans-Peter laughed. Because Kim has never in his life required shoelaces it was difficult for Hans-Peter to explain to him what had tripped him.

A lucky fall

From this day on, Kirsten's image of her "Kimmi" changed forever. He was no longer the awkward, boorish Haflinger who knocked her off her feet, swept her spectacles off her nose, who barged into her and against whose atrocities she had to be continually on guard. This horse was strong but he was well aware of his strength and could precisely—to within millimeters—control his body. From that day on Kirsten, too, could play with Kim—carefree and unrestrained.

A horse that learns to know himself also learns to master himself. Horses can and want to understand our vulnerability. They know what it is to be afraid. Of course, for our part, we have to lay open our weaknesses rather than bury them in a dominant approach. A horse that is master of himself is an absolutely reliable partner: it is, after all, about togetherness, about friendship. How did that go again? The weaker partner determines the intensity of the game, the stronger one is considerate of the weaker. Kim has changed and he now senses what Kirsten fears. Of his own accord he maintains a greater distance, for safety's sake, when he is with her in the arena than when he is with others. His games with Kirsten are always more subdued and not as "close to the bone" as with other people. He does not want to alarm her in any way. Kim, all on his own, takes Kirsten's unique needs into consideration regardless of how wild his own mood is, even though she never asked him for this.

On the concept of considerateness

The Thing about Riding

Human beings are different! They need special, gentle games because every single horse is superior to them in physical strength and speed. They have special ideas that can give a horse a completely new awareness of his body—perhaps even to the point that the horse has never felt so strong! Human beings can help a horse concentrate his balance. They help him make his movement conscious. This is all new, and it is not at all typical for horses—just like riding.

There is no natural circumstance in the life of a horse that even remotely resembles the experience of being ridden. By the time of the first mounting, at the latest, the human being will have become someone completely "the other" to the horse. In nature, this arrangement would represent the threatening grip of a predator on the horse's back. The fear-evoking quality of this situation becomes stronger the more threatening the horse finds the proximity of the person.

On rules of play and horse psychology

There is no such thing as "natural riding." Riding, except as a predator on the back and neck, never occurs anywhere in a horse's natural world. A human being is not a harmless sparrow that perches on a horse's croup for a few moments. There is no such thing as "horse-like" riding. If riding is to be a pleasant experience for both parties it must arise out of the special relationship between horse and person. Only a human being lets himself be carried by a horse. Only a horse allows a person the experience of riding. Our experiences

The First Rider

Intrigued, young Shane approaches when the woman cracks the whip. "Maybe she has another one of her interesting ideas. Yes, she does!" She jumps up onto his back, cavorts around up there, is overjoyed by the whole situation and totally enthusiastic. Then she slides down back to the ground. What very odd behavior—but she seems to think it is so super that one sees oneself as totally super too.

Here is a young stallion confronted for the first time with a rider's weight on his back. He stands quietly during this totally new experience, he does not move one foot during all my activity, except to place his legs further apart to better deal with the unaccustomed weight. This is not some new technique for a first ride! It is playful gymnastics for half a minute. Shane will not experience anything similar for a long time to come. But, one day in the future he may remember this unusual experience and the proud feeling he had.

A Common Language

"Hey, Hazel! Come play with me, catch me...! What's the matter sweetheart? What's wrong? Don't you want to play with me...?" At this point in the conversation, Hans-Peter turned to me. "What does she want?" I suggested to him to try riding. He let himself be talked into it, but only reluctantly.

"Hmmm...How do I get up there? I don't just want to jump on your back."

"Just do it!" and "There you are...finally!" Hazel seems to say.

Immediately after this dialog, a horse-and-rider pair emerges, totally absorbed in one another to a degree seldom seen. Hans-Peter listens to his horse; he concentrates fully on Hazel. He is open, loose, feeling, and because of that, his body position is so communicative that the horse receives the confirmation she needs. This is why the mare can carry him and herself as lightly as a feather. Note the position of Hazel's ears and her relaxed lips. The aura of the two of them is soft, round, centered, intense—a beautiful, harmonious picture. A few minutes later Hans-Peter is again a bit hesitant and so disrupts the mental connection. This is how he suddenly finds his "feel" more on than "in" his horse. The direct contact he had at first, that listening "into" Hazel, has got somewhat lost. "What's the matter?" Hazel's look seems to ask. Hans-Peter tries to recreate the lost contact by using his hands—a totally natural reaction for us. Our hands are our most important sensory organs and we also gladly use them in communicating with other human beings when spoken language does not suffice. Establishing contact, greeting, sympathy, empathy—all these are expressed with the hands among people. It is different with horses, so for a while the two of them stand there and do not quite know what to do next. The whip that I give Hans-Peter does not help. Hans-Peter is irritated by it—he does not want anything like that, and for

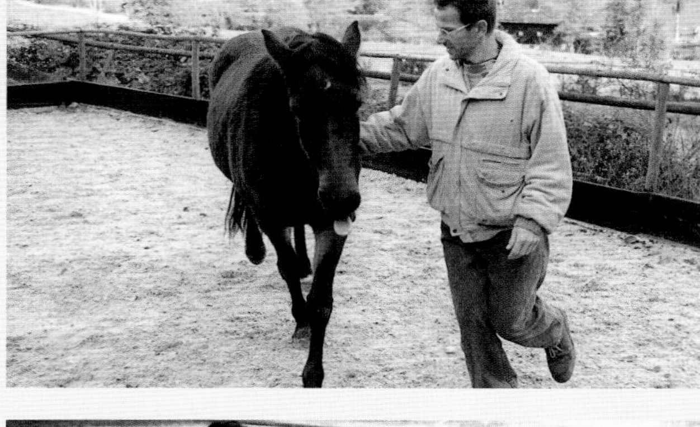

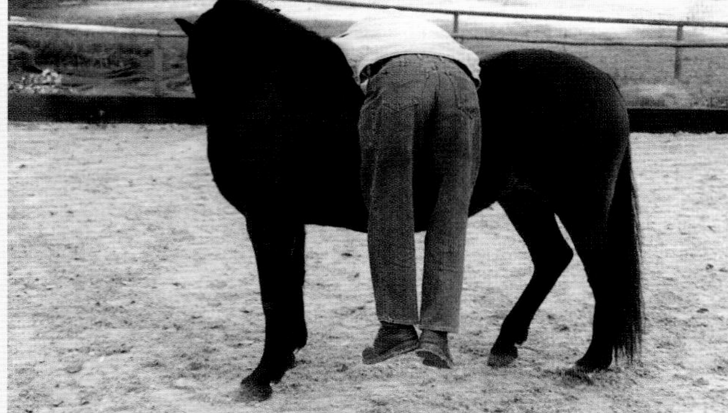

the rest of the session he moves it out of his way, pinning it under his arm. "Hands on horse" works much better.

Hazel begins to adjust to this unaccustomed form of communication and adapts to the fact that her newly chosen rider is still thinking a bit "forehand-ish" at the moment. The two of them attempt their first trot together. I run alongside for a bit, but Hazel concentrates completely on her rider and there, in the first turn, she puts this inexperienced rider in exactly the correct position for going smoothly into the bend. Loose, well-balanced, and as though poured from the same mold, the two of them trot out of the corner. Hazel has made her Hans-Peter a rider. Can you see in the last photo how Hazel still "listens" to Hans-Peter's right hand? Even though Hans-Peter's attention is now on us observers rather than fully on her, Hazel attentively maintains the connection to her passenger.

Riding is not natural!

doing this can be so unique and extraordinary that for the rest of our lives we can never again be without horses. And this same unique and extraordinary feeling is something horses can experience too.

Leading, saddling, riding—because these activities are so atypical for a horse, it is especially important that they develop in a playful and spontaneous way, in a protected atmosphere, and with the horse's agreement. That is how Kirsten introduced young Shannon to the saddle for the first time, and that is how I sit on Shane for the first time. I think we understand each other: what you see in the photos on page 177 is not some new technique for "breaking" a horse. A very special, unique horse and a very special, unique person are doing something together that precisely suits both of them at this moment.

It is an agenda-free, playful action, even though it does, of course, have a deeper significance. The relationship between us is the decisive factor. The horse listens backward and trusts in me, even when I behave in a most extraordinary way behind him and on his back. The young stallion would not permit his friend Shannon such an action. Were Shannon to try "riding" him, Shane would duck away, turn with lightening speed and grab his friend with his teeth, and right away a great romp would take place. Even if herd boss Toppur were to try such a thing, a similar sequence of events would occur. But then, I am not a horse. So, Shane permits me the gymnastics, and in the end he is also mightily proud of himself.

You are different!

A Taste of Carrots

"There she is!" The young chestnut gelding's head jerks up, he leaves the herd and runs excitedly back and forth along the fence. "There's Steffi...there she comes!" His Steffi.

"Hello, Kveikur!" she calls to him. Then she goes into the rider's cabin to arm herself with whip and carrots, while Kveikur stands at the gate, trembling with excitement. Steffi lets him out and he greets her effusively. "Just a second, Kveikur, let me just close the gate. It's okay now. I know you had to wait. I had so much to do for school, but now it's your turn." The two of them run to the arena. Kveikur circles around the girl, she runs ahead, he chases her, they dodge and feint, play catch. The little Icelandic horse always wins. When Steffi is out of breath and can't run anymore, she swings herself up onto his back. Kveikur enthusiastically turns his head as he hears Steffi breaking off a piece of carrot up there. Again they make their circles, stop, race off...only now Kveikur has his Steffi "piggyback."

The two of them enjoy their time together—sometimes silly, sometimes concentrating intently, sometimes wild and fast, sometimes quiet, soft, thoughtful. Pretty as a picture the pair trots past, then suddenly Kveikur hops madly around, spinning like a young dog chasing its tail. The wild rushing and jumping is enough to make an observer's heart stop, but Steffi calmly accepts the bronco-like leaps: "So what if he's bucking, "she laughs contentedly. "It's not against me! He's bucking with me!"

The Active Horse

Everything we do with a horse takes place within a certain specific framework. If this framework is defined by the supremacy or dominance of the human being, then every single action will have an entirely different meaning than if it were performed within a framework of friendship. There is a fundamental difference between someone successfully managing to get into our home without being asked, and our inviting and welcoming him in. To us, a "home invader" is not at all like an invited guest. A horse views things exactly

The welcome rider

the same way. Riding can be a forceful intrusion, but it can also come about because of the horse's hospitality—all depending on the circumstances. A horse that seeks out his rider and wants to be close to him will feel encouraged to step under the weight of the person and carry him, practically of his own accord. On the other hand, a horse that feels oppressed by the rider will pull away, avoid the burden, and try to run from it. The horse's "yes" is the key here—riding by invitation.

It was a lucky coincidence that Hans-Peter's ride (see p. 178) was so well-documented because we did not "stage" anything here. I would like to tell you how this group of images came to be.

Hazel is obstinate

A horse and a person were together in the arena and Hans-Peter thought Hazel wanted to play with him, as often happens. But the games he offered were not what Hazel wanted. He had run off in an attempt to enliven her. "I think she wants you to ride her," I said, and we laughed as Hans-Peter at first indignantly rejected this suggestion.

"I don't need to ride. I can walk on my own...that's what my legs are for! No one has to carry me!"

We laughed because it was clear who would win here: Hans-Peter's resistance was futile, because Hazel did not play along. Or, much more to the point, she knew exactly what she wanted...and she persisted. All the choices Hans-Peter presented were met with total disinterest. Instead of joining in with his attempts, Hazel turned her back to him, or more accurately, presented the side of her body...and waited. Finally Hans-Peter admitted defeat. The mare had convinced him and so he found himself on Hazel's back—for the first time ever.

Hans-Peter's "feel"

The photo series is highly interesting because it not only shows us the sequence of events but also lets us see the effect of "mere thoughts." At first, the two have a very good emotional connection. Hans-Peter listens "into" the horse and Hazel relishes her victory. Then Hans-Peter gradually thinks himself into believing that he does not know how to ride and should learn that first and that Hazel surely must be expecting more of him. I give him the whip so that he has help keeping contact, but he accepts it only half-heartedly. This tool, universally seen in the negative sense as an instrument to force compliance, seems sinister to him; he wants nothing to do with it. "What do you want with that?" an astonished Hazel asks him, and slightly confused and ill at ease, Hans-Peter promptly puts away under his arm this item that was forced on him—after all, he neither wanted to ride nor use a whip! The two of them rediscover their secure connection with one another as I walk along beside them for a little while. Hazel begins to understand that Hans-Peter's primary way of feeling is through his hands and she empathetically goes along. In a short time, she is able to carry him with momentum and rhythm through a turn. She helps Hans-Peter to better sense himself and her, and to feel more centered and secure.

When riding, there is direct permanent contact that neither participant can avoid. This contact can only be dissolved when the rider dismounts or falls off. For that reason, on the horse's back, courteous behavior ought to be a matter of course: we should wait for an invitation, ask permission, request rather than demand, and do our best to adapt ourselves. Horses know to appreciate such restraint from a human being and they become thoughtful, considerate, solicitous hosts.

Hospitality and Feel for a Language

Riding with the horse's permission is not a high-low relationship, even though the person is sitting on the horse. Purely superficially the person "possesses" the horse's back, and that can be irritating to the rider even when he, like Hans-Peter, has no pretensions to a

Awareness through touch: we walked backward together and Hazel maintained contact to her right hindquarter because she felt my hand there. It would be so much better if I could be on both sides of the horse at the same time…

…like here! Now that I am on Hazel's back, we have contact over a much greater surface area. When Hazel concentrates on the person's touch she goes automatically to her own center rather than shifting her center of gravity off to one side. Her attention wanders into herself. Hazel can no longer see me. Because we can barely see each other in this situation our communication shifts to "feel," and no matter how fast the mare moves, I am always with her, close as her skin.

Why the whip?

horse-breaker's grand gestures. We humans, too, must first become accustomed to the neutral power relationship and so redefine a number of things for ourselves. We discover that the whip, a threatening instrument and a scepter of power in a hierarchical relationship, can in an intimate, trusting space, be a useful aid in facilitating understanding between man and horse. In an environment where human beings hold all the power, the whip will always be an instrument of punishment, even if the rider never uses it. In an intimate trusting relationship we communicate equal to equal and the connection created with the help of the whip can convey concentration and help us bring power to the right spot. The whip makes energy tangible, improves the connection, and helps the person who is acting for the benefit of the horse express himself more clearly.

"Riding is a practical, strenuous, cultivating form of love."
~Heimito von Doderer

In the previous chapters, we saw how critical it is for a horse to see our activities as helpful and interesting, and to enthusiastically welcome them, if they are to have a positive effect. The horse does not avoid contact, rather, he seeks it. If a person works in accord with positive principles, he will have a horse that welcomes the presence of human beings. Such a person does not drive his horse away so he does not have to hold him back. He does not take himself too seriously and also does not demand that his horse does. His horse can carry him without worries. Hans-Peter does not sit on the horse like a typical beginning rider—lonesome up there on a precarious unstable base. His emotional space includes Hazel. He long ago went beyond the visible physical boundaries of his body—he had a "feeling" with the mare long before he sat on her back for the first time. The close physical contact is not frightening for either of them because their intimate awareness of one another had already been in full swing.

The joy of connection and open boundaries

To a horse that has learned to appreciate the assistance of a human being, riding is simply an intensification of what he has been doing all along. Yes, he even sees it as a splendid idea to carry his person on his back because during their walks together the two-legged one always falls behind, so that the horse must wait for him if he does not want to lose him. At some point it becomes very matter of course to the horse that riding will evolve out of the friendship with the person—even if only because of the balance of power. In addition, the person is knowledgeable about the human world out there and literally covers the four-legged one's back. On the other hand, in a horse's own territory, a place where he feels safe, the idea of riding seems useful in a different way. In the photos of Hazel we can see why: as soon as Hans-Peter's concentration wanders down to—and he tries to feel her through—his "hips and haunches," the horse can do the same thing. As soon as Hans-Peter takes up the connection to Hazel through his seat, the mare senses her own hindquarters more. This is the reason why the seat always plays such a central role in classical riding art: a person who concentrates on his seat makes it possible for the horse to purposefully collect himself.

Riding in friendship

The Interesting Human Being

Good riding is an art that is very difficult to learn. A person has to feel the horse and his own body in motion: Where is his balance? What rhythm does he prefer? How is he placing his feet? How and where is he moving his center of gravity? This is not so easy to grasp and requires decades of experience. In normal day-to-day human activity seat and thighs are not required to perceive and respond to foreign ways of moving. We need a special power of perception for the art of riding that I call a "listening seat." What can greatly help us to develop this sensitivity is our kinesthetic sense—the image of movement we create for ourselves when we are in an intense exchange with a horse while working on the ground. If we are emotionally involved as we observe our horse, it will improve this sense

Good riding is sensitive

The Conquering Horse

Running away and capturing: Kim carefully considers Kirsten's particular circumstances: while he plays with her he maintains a good distance between them. Someone like Kirsten who is anxious needs more space. Or, perhaps this horse is simply settling the dominance issue! In the end—just like a real round-pen expert—he has Kirsten willingly "joining-up" and "following closely." We cannot escape from these empowered horses!

and we intuitively begin to give the right movement in response.

The path that is described here makes our learning process much easier. We have on our side a horse that feels good, has accepted us as a playmate, and is on the same level with us. He comes to meet us instead of running away. He understands our aids as an expression of solicitousness, affection, and responsibility, even when they are occasionally clumsy. We do not have to be perfect. I too first learned to ride correctly like this—from the horse, not from famous teachers. The communicative horse will clearly let us know what he sees as positive and what not, because he trusts that we will listen to him and take heed of what he tells us. We can be truly supportive to this horse because he communicates with us—we have not trained him to be a tolerant subordinate. So, we can give him aids to carry himself differently because he has integrated us into his social network. We can show him the way into new patterns of movement to give him a sense of how it feels to carry his weight on the haunches.

Learning from one another

When horse and rider achieve mental oneness and the horse does not perceive the rider as a "foreign body," the horse will balance the rider very precisely. Then, even turns and powerful leaps will not endanger their mutual balance. Reno taking off into levade, Kveikur bucking and spinning, Hazel going into a turn with Hans-Peter: a horse that wants his rider up there will put him in the proper position. The rider can relax and stay loose—the horse has incorporated him into his own body awareness.

Why do these horses want this? What is it about us that they find so interesting? Leaving aside the fact that we might have treats in our pockets, horses appreciate our ability to come up with good ideas. Horses are creatures of habit and will stay on their old familiar track—they are very linear that way. Human beings recognize pattern and possibilities and can encourage horses to explore new tracks. So, horses become more flexible and expand their movement repertoire, as a consequence of which they can also better adapt to their altered life circumstances. Basically, the subject of this book is nothing other than how to support and help the horse in his quest to perfect himself. Horses are by nature a bit "uncentered," unfocused—already in part because of their wide-angled, diffuse way of seeing the world—and they benefit from the ability of human beings to concentrate. Riding, in particular, can serve the purpose of leading the horse back into himself. By way of the "detour" of the rider, the horse feels his own body more: assuming of course that this is a horse that wants to be with me and is not merely yielding or submitting because he has been trained using fear. When I disappear from his field of vision by getting on his back, the horse feels more, and the act of feeling and listening to the rider becomes listening into his own body!

"Flexible fit" for an unfamiliar situation

Through this close connection with a human being the horse experiences himself in a new way. In the continuous checking-in with and inquiring after his rider, he is continuously checking-in with and inquiring after himself, expanding his own physical space as he makes the rider part of his own body awareness. He feels strong and proud in the encounter. The process that we call collection plays a decisive role in this. Collection as a process of teamwork with the human being unlocks additional powers for the horse. He discovers potential in himself that was not accessible until now. As we noted before, collected movement does occur in nature. However, collection in our way of working is far more than that. In this work with a human being a horse's natural abilities are cultivated. In the language of horses, collected movement signifies play, self-confidence, and impressiveness—empowerment. Whether or not a horse living in the wild comes into this state depends on external circumstances and his behavior, too, is directed toward the outside, to external circumstances. In our work, collection is a path inward. This collection makes the horse himself the center, the focal point. Play, fighting, impressing others—these situ-

Opportunities for collection

For a moment the close confines are forgotten, and Pegasus, the magic winged steed of ancient times, comes alive before our eyes. The power of joy gives him form: even in a world filled with fences, he is free in spirit.

ations are coincidental. A horse that has learned to consciously collect himself can summon up collected movements at will, and can get the good feelings connected with them independent of external circumstances.

The Power of Imagination

Inspiration gives horses wings

We human beings have the power to reach horses emotionally. Instead of interacting destructively, using our inheritance of dominance to break the horse's spirit, we can use our power in a new and inspiring way for the benefit of our horses. The horse trotting sadly along is not able to think up a proud trot for himself. We humans have our imagination with which we can visualize a life beyond the pressure and stress that oppress us at the moment. With our vision of the ideal we can, step-by-step, leave our cares behind, and so free our spirits. A horse cannot do this. He is far more bound to his body and caught in the experience of the moment. He cannot find a mental escape from the oppression of the here and now. With the help of our power of visualization the horse gradually gains a new

Our journey together has come to an end. Just as I had let Toppur go back to his pasture, he suddenly sprinted up the hill next to me, "What's the matter? Don't you want to go back to your herd?" It looks almost as though he wants me to stay. After all, there is plenty of grass for everyone. "I can't do that Toppur. I have to leave now. You know, I'm writing a book about all of you, because there are still many people who want to know about your world." He does not seem entirely satisfied with that answer...

Riding and the lightness of being

awareness of himself. The person's imagination provides the stimulus and can inspire the horse to discover a free path to his body. Given wings by the presence of his human friend, the horse becomes light, nimble, powerful, and bursting with energy. He breaks free from his inner shackles and liberates himself from his habitual track. We stimulate horses; we encourage their unfolding process, their creativity, their transformation—until they are able to find their art form from within themselves.

In classical riding art there is a French term that describes the ideal condition of the ridden horse: *légèreté* or "lightness." Such a horse is unblocked and without excess tension; he moves fluidly, expressively and regally. In the specialized equestrian language of modern dressage this concept has changed in a very specific way. In German we have *Durchlässigkeit.* In English, we sometimes choose to use this German word, but more often use the translation, "throughness." We mean by that a horse that is open and permeable to the aids, who lets them go through his whole body; in other words, a horse that does not offer any resistance to his rider's commands. Total responsiveness, a sense of duty, and the careful and conscientious utilization of horseflesh were all part of a riding tradition defined by its military background. But lightness of spirit? Feeling carefree, feeling joy? *Légèreté* is difficult to incorporate into the world of command and obey. However, today we no longer have to wage war from the backs of our horses. I believe that in our day we have, for the first time, the opportunity to experience something with our horses of which our forefathers could only dream—simply because we no longer need the horse for war, agriculture, or transportation.

In past times, the utility aspect was the most important reason for man's interaction with the horse, and it defined their relationship. But now our horse himself can become the reason for our work together. In our time we have the opportunity to participate in a new art form, one that is totally devoted to the horse. Instead of coming up with new tasks that force him into doing something for our sport, entertainment, and leisure time enjoyment, we can, at the very least, give something back: freedom in being together with us.

We can release him, and in his company, we ourselves can become more "through": open, permeable, and responsive to the momentum and rhythm of feelings, to the flow of life's energy—the lightness of being.

Closing Remarks from Reno

I do not hesitate to step in here and have my say. I have learned how urgent it is to get your ear, to get your full attention, just as I have learned that there is no exit for us and freedom is a dream that belongs forever to the past. Were it otherwise, I would fly free as the wind over the prairie grass, with those I love gathered around me.

The ideas I would like to put before you arose in a lively exchange of thoughts with my esteemed colleagues, all of them civilized horses like me. We know that we have no choice, that our captivity is permanent, irrevocable. We are speaking with you because we know that. The possibility of reconciliation is a principle of every culture. Reconciliation is communication with the ones with whom we have differences, with the ones who are different in order to come to an understanding. Communication in that spirit is the subject of this book. It is not enough merely to wait for enlightenment to come to you or to hope that the animals of this world survive the evils perpetrated by the human race. We must speak with you.

I plead for a culture of the heart in which horses and human beings agree to come together with the best that they can bring to one another: courtesy, affection, trust, love—everything that enriches life and makes it seem more worth living, even though there is no true freedom anymore.

For a long time we horses believed that giving humans this best of ourselves would be an effective solution. This was a painful error. Giving you our best has not saved us from conflict: it has not saved us from the lash of the whip, the ropes and shackles, or from being put behind bars. This best of ourselves is most often simply overlooked.

We horses must now take a roundabout way, a path that leads through "technique," in the broadest sense of the word. This is a technique for coming to mutual understanding in a polite way, a technique of communication that masters even the problematical human race. Informing you of this technique and demonstrating it is my contribution to this book.

~Written down for Reno by
Hans-Peter Gerstner

About the Author & the Horses

Even as a child Imke Spilker was fascinated with horses, but the human-horse relationship always seemed to her to be too one-sided. It saddened her that happiness was not mutual—that the rider's good feelings usually came at the expense of the horse. "Is there anything we can give horses in return for what they have given us?" This is the question that subsequently guided her life

Imke Spilker is a linguist who studied language sciences at Heidelberg in Germany. Always in search of the truth of the horse behind the great words of human beings, she has immersed herself in the works of the old masters of equitation. Partnership, harmony, beauty, freedom—can we transmit these concept to the horse in such a way that he actually understands our intention? Or must he remain raw material, to be shaped according to the rider's conception of art?

Fifteen years ago, Imke Spilker found four-legged teachers who answered these questions—under saddle and in the pasture. With these horses she founded the Communicative Horses Project (www.kommunikativepferde.de). In this project, horses have their say. The horses learn to "whisper" to human beings, while humans learn how to listen to their horses and come into a true conversation with them. This book, *Empowered Horses*, evolved from work of the Communicative Horses Project.

This book could not have come to be without the extraordinary effort and engagement of all the horses in our project. Special participation was offered by:
Atila, Lusitano; Batist, HalflingerXWelsh; El Paso, Riding Pony; Gl. Charming Hazel, Connemara; Gl. Gentle Joy, Connemara; Kim, Haflinger; Kveikur, Icelandic; Max, Bosnian; Passaro, Arabian; Reno, WelshXArabian; Stonebrook Gentle Jocey, Connemara; Stonebrook Charming Sean, Connemara; Stonebrook Gentle Shane, Connemara; Stonebrook Charming Shannon, Connemara; Toppur, Icelandic

Index

Page numbers in *italic* indicate photographs.